An Occult Guide to the Tarot

By Waite, Ouspensky, Thierens, and Papus

Edited by Travis McHenry

An Occult Guide to the Tarot
Waite, Ouspensky, Thierens, and Papus
Travis McHenry, Ed.

© 2015 Travis McHenry

FIRST EDITION

ISBN: 978-1-329-79779-6

Table of Contents

Introduction

It is a difficult thing to create a cohesive guide that covers the totality of the Tarot. Since the creation of the first known Tarot decks in the early 1400s, each successive deck has been created using symbols and philosophies which have evolved and sometimes diverged from the previous generation of cards. The meanings of the symbols on the cards are secondary to the divinatory meanings inherent in the cards themselves—the symbols serve as a guide to remind the cartomancer what each card represents. It is only through a higher understanding of astrology, occult knowledge, and ancient Kabalistic symbology that the true meaning of the cards can be comprehended and utilized for divination purposes, because it is from these sources that the Tarot acquires its meaning.

The study of these subjects could take a lifetime to master entirely. Fortunately, for the beginning cartomancer, there are four texts that provide basic knowledge about the esoteric origins of the Tarot:

The Pictorial Key to the Tarot by A.E Waite (1911)

The Symbolism of the Tarot by P.D. Ouspensky (1913)

General Book of the Tarot by A.E. Thierens (1928)

The Tarot of the Bohemians by Papus, Translated by A.P. Morton (1892)

The level of detail found in these four books is sufficient to reveal the divinatory message of Tarot readings, but the four authors frequently contradict one another, and especially in the case of Papus, the symbolic meanings become lost in a haze of esoteric hieroglyphics intended for specialists of occult symbology. As the creator of the most popular Tarot deck of the past 100 years—the Rider-Waite-Smith Deck—A.E. Waite's *The Pictorial Key to the Tarot* has served as a baseline for divinatory meanings behind the cards. However, Waite fails to explain how he arrived at his meanings, leaving the cartomancer to trust that Waite's suggestions are applicable for all readings, when in fact they are only general indications of each card's significance. To further understand how Waite devised his divinations and created the symbols for the cards, Thierens' and Papus' texts map out the astrological and occult connotations of the Tarot. Ouspensky's dreamlike narrative journey through the Tarot has been added as a postlude in italics to further explore the imagery found in the illustrations of the Major Arcana.

This book serves as a judiciously edited amalgamation of these four works into one cohesive volume. It is intended as a compendium of divinatory meanings, their symbolic origins in astrology and the occult, and a cross-reference of Tarot decks from the 1400s until the present.

-TRAVIS MCHENRY

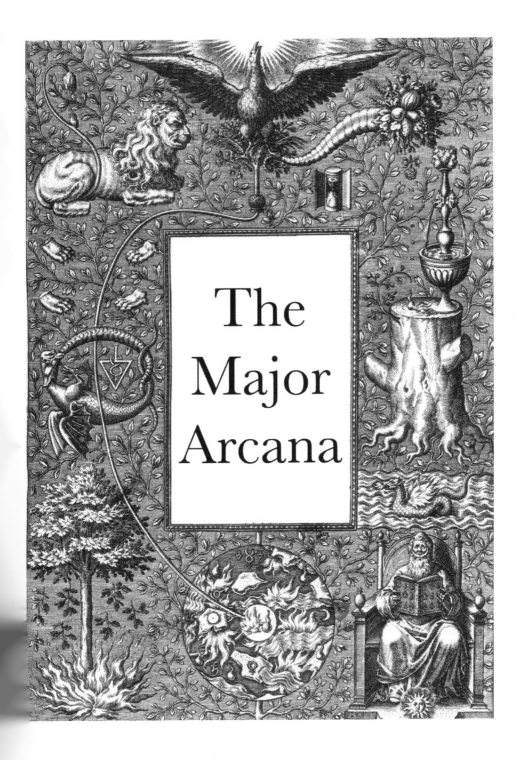

The Major Arcana

Card O – The Fool

Divinatory Meanings: Folly, mania, extravagance, intoxication, delirium, frenzy, betrayal.

Reversed: Negligence, absence, distribution, carelessness, apathy, nullity, vanity.

The Fool, *Mate*, or *Unwise Man* signifies the flesh, the sensitive life, and by a peculiar satire its subsidiary name was at one time the alchemist, as depicting folly at the most insensate stage. This is an image of the state to which unresisted passion will reduce a man. It is the symbol of the Flesh and of its gratification.

With light step, as if Earth had little power to restrain him, a young man in gorgeous vestments pauses at the brink of a precipice among the great heights of the world; he surveys the blue distance before him—its expanse of sky, rather than the prospect below. The edge which opens on the depth has no terror; it is as if angels were waiting to uphold him if he leaped from the height. His countenance is full of intelligence and expectant dream. He has a rose in one hand and in the other a costly wand, from which suspends over his right shoulder an embroidered wallet. He is a prince of the other world on his travels through this one—all amidst the morning glory. The sun, which shines behind him, knows whence he came, whither he is going, and how he will return by another path after many days. He is the spirit in search of experience.

Although it is sometimes inserted as card 21, Court de Gebelin—an 18th century French esoteric philosopher—places it at the head of the whole series as the zero or negative which is presupposed by numeration, and as this is simpler, so it is also a better arrangement. The Fool carries a wallet; he is looking over his shoulder and does not know that he is on the brink of a precipice; but a dog or other animal—some call it a tiger —is attacking him from behind, and he is hurried to his destruction unawares. There is also a justifiable variation of this card in the form of a court jester—with cap, bells and motley garb. The other descriptions say that the wallet contains the bearer's follies and vices, which seems bourgeois and arbitrary.

To us, creatures living upon the Earth, this globe cannot be observed by us from outside, and The Fool is represented as a man walking without paying attention to himself. There is something of absolute Fate about this figure, which reminds us of the old saying of astrologers: "The wise man rules his stars, the fool obeys them." On the point of this fatality all authorities agree. The planets give us the symbols or ideas of organs of consciousness, the zodiacal signs denote modes of substance, from which consciousness is derived. So the *zero*-principle is the symbol of *un*consciousness. In fact he who is unconscious, of himself or of Self, will obey every intimation from without and obeys his stars—his senses, stupidly, blindly.

Of course this card has much to do with foolishness, spiritual dumbness, but it bears also the meaning of that which cannot be helped; or that which will come right of itself and need not be heeded by us: that to which we are subject, as to the Earth's course in its orbit. It does not need our personal assistance. Realizing the latter fact this Fool might after all appear to be wiser than a good many other people, who in their human vanity imagine they are greatly needed for carrying out the intentions of their God, of whom they claim a personal knowledge. A proverb says that children and fools tell the truth.

Tired and lame he dragged himself along the dusty road, across the deserted plain under the scorching rays of the sun. He glanced sidelong with foolish, staring eyes, a half smile on his face; he knew not where he went, but was absorbed in his dreams which ran constantly in the same circle. His fool's cap was put on wrong side front and his garments were torn in the back. All the time holding on his shoulder a bag containing the four magic symbols, the wand, the cup, the sword, and the pentacle. The Fool always carries them, although he has long since forgotten what they mean. Nevertheless they belong to him, even though he does not know their use.

Card I – The Magician

Divinatory Meanings: Skill, diplomacy, subtlety. Sickness, pain, loss, disaster, snares of enemies. Self-confidence, will. The Querent, if male.
Reversed: Physician, mental disease, disgrace, disquiet.

The Magus, Magician, or *Juggler*, the caster of the dice and deceiver, in the world of vulgar trickery. A youthful figure in the robe of a magician with smile of confidence and shining eyes. Above his head is the mysterious sign of the Holy Spirit, the sign of life, like an endless cord, forming the figure 8 in a horizontal position. Around his waist is an Ouroboros—the serpent devouring its own tail. This is familiar to most as a conventional symbol of eternity, but here it indicates more especially the eternity of attainment in the spirit. In the Magician's right hand is a wand raised towards heaven, while the left hand is pointing to the earth. This dual sign shows the descent of grace, virtue, and light, drawn from things above and derived to things below. The suggestion throughout is therefore the possession and communication of the Powers and Gifts of the Spirit.

On the table in front of the Magician are the symbols of the four Tarot suits, signifying the elements of natural life, which lie like counters before the adept, and he adapts them as he wills. Beneath are roses and lilies, the *flos campi* and *lilium convallium*, changed into garden flowers, to show the culture of aspiration. This card signifies the divine motive in man, reflecting God, the will in the liberation of its union with that which is above. The Magician should rule the month of Aries.

His figure reached from earth to heaven and was clad in a purple mantle. He stood deep in foliage and flowers. His head, on which was the head-band of an initiate, seemed to disappear mysteriously in infinity. I saw myself reflected in him as in a mirror and in his eyes I seemed to look upon myself. With his hands he unites heaven and earth, and the four elements that form the world are controlled by him. The four symbols before him are the four letters of the name of God, the signs of the four elements, fire, water, air, earth.

Card II – The High Priestess

Divinatory Meanings: Secrets, mystery, the future as yet unrevealed. The woman who interests the Querent, if male. The Querent herself, if female. Silence, tenacity. Mystery, wisdom, science.

Reversed: Passion, moral or physical ardor, conceit, surface knowledge.

The High Priestess, Pope Joan, or *Female Pontiff* is sometimes held to represent the Divine Law and the Gnosis. She has the lunar crescent at her feet, a horned diadem on her head, with a globe in the middle place, and a large solar cross on her breast. The scroll in her hands is inscribed with the word *Tora*, signifying the Greater Law, the Secret Law, and the second sense of the Word. It is partly covered by her mantle, to show that some things are implied and some spoken. She is seated between the white and black pillars (B. and J.) of the mystic Temple, and the veil of the Temple is behind her: it is embroidered with palms and pomegranates. The vestments are flowing and gauzy, and the mantle suggests light—a shimmering radiance.

The initials stand for Boaz and Jachin which were two pillars that stood in the porch of Solomon's Temple, the first Temple in Jerusalem. Boaz stood on the left and Jachin stood on the right. The two pillars measured nearly six feet thick and 27 feet tall. The eight-foot-high brass capitals on top of the columns bore decorations of brass lilies. The original measurement as taken from the Bible was in cubits, which states that the pillars were 18 cubits high and 12 cubits around; and hollow, four fingers thick (Jeremiah 52:21-22). Nets of check-work covered the bowl of each capital, decorated with rows of two hundred pomegranates, and wreathed with seven chains for each capital, and topped with lilies (1 Kings 7:13-22, 41-42).

The High Priestess symbolizes constancy, fidelity, repose, stability, but also dumbness, laziness, resistance, and endurance, as well as passive opposition. It rules everything in connection with art and the artistic abilities, with wealth and with the masonic lodge. She has been called *occult Science on the threshold of the Sanctuary of Isis*, but she is really the Secret Church, the House which is of God and man. She represents also the Second Marriage of the Prince who is no longer of this world; she is the spiritual Bride and Mother, the daughter of the stars and the Higher Garden of Eden. There are some respects in which this card is the highest and holiest of the Major Arcana.

The Magician represents a man standing—The High Priestess, on the contrary, bears the figure of a seated woman. The man, endowed with all the attributes of power, was placed in the midst of nature. The woman is adorned with all the attributes of authority and persuasion, and she is placed under the porch of the temple of Isis, between two columns.

When I lifted the first veil and entered the outer court of the Temple of Initiation, I saw in half darkness the figure of a woman sitting on a high throne between two pillars of the temple, one white, and one black. Mystery emanated from her and was about her. "To enter the Temple one must lift the second veil and pass between the two pillars. And to pass thus, one must obtain possession of the keys, read the book, and understand the symbols. Are you able to do this?" Then the woman turned her face to me and looked into my eyes without speaking. And through me passed a thrill, mysterious and penetrating like a golden wave; tones vibrated in my brain, a flame was in my heart, and I understood that she spoke to me, saying without words: "This is the Hall of Wisdom. No one can reveal it, no one can hide it. Like a flower it must grow and bloom in thy soul."

Card III – The Empress

Divinatory Meanings: Fruitfulness, fertility, action, initiative, length of days. The unknown, clandestine. Difficulty, doubt, ignorance.

Reversed: Light, truth, the unravelling of involved matters, public rejoicings.

The Empress has been connected with the ideas of universal fertility and in a general sense, with activity. A stately figure, seated, having rich vestments and royal aspect, as a daughter of heaven and earth. Her diadem is of twelve stars, gathered in a cluster. The symbol of Venus is on the shield which rests near her. A field of corn is ripening in front of her, and beyond there is a fall of water. The scepter which she bears is surmounted by the globe of this world. She is the inferior Garden of Eden, the Earthly Paradise, all that is symbolized by the visible house of man.

There are also certain aspects in which she has been correctly described as desire and the wings thereof, as the woman clothed with the sun. She is above all things universal fertility and the outer sense of the Word. This is obvious, because there is no direct message which has been given to man like that which is borne by woman; but she does not herself carry its interpretation.

The Empress is indeed a daughter of Heaven and Earth, for she represents the sphere of Mercury, Messenger of the Gods, and so this card always bears the meaning of messages and writing, and of news to be heard, instructions to be received. Twelve (in older pictures nine) stars are placed around her head and this means that the messages come to us from the stars. One of the older editions shows the Empress holding in her left hand a wand with a heraldic lily with a trefoil on its top, very suggestive of the origin of the color or suit of wands, which has a close relation with the card of Gemini.

In the midst of a green meadow where primroses bloomed, I saw the Empress seated on a throne covered with ivy and lilacs. "Queen of life," I said, "How can you smile so joyfully on the opening flowers, when everything is destined to death, even that which has not yet been born?" For answer the Empress looked on me still smiling and, under the influence of that smile, I suddenly felt a flower of some clear understanding open in my heart.

Card IV – The Emperor

Divinatory Meanings: Stability, power, protection. A great person. Aid, reason, conviction. Authority and will. The father of the Querent. The past and tradition.

Reversed: Benevolence, compassion, credit. Confusion to enemies, obstruction, immaturity.

The Emperor is occasionally represented as wearing, in addition to his personal insignia, the stars or ribbons of some order of chivalry. For his scepter, he has a form of the *Crux ansata* (a symbol of the might of inner life, which rules matter) and a globe in his left hand. In different editions of the card there are different sorts of scepters in the hand of the Emperor. In some there appears also an eagle. He is a crowned monarch—commanding, stately, seated on a throne, the arms of which are fronted by rams' heads. His crown has twelve points signifying the overruling power of the Zodiac. He is executive and realization, the power of this world, here clothed with the highest of its natural attributes. He is the virile power, to which the Empress responds, and in this sense is he who seeks to remove the Veil of Isis; yet she remains *virgo intacta*.

It should be understood that this card and that of the Empress do not precisely represent the condition of married life, though this state is implied. On the surface, they stand for mundane royalty, uplifted on the seats of the mighty; but above this there is the suggestion of another presence. They signify also—and the male figure especially—the higher kingship, occupying the intellectual throne. Theirs is the lordship of thought rather than of the animal world.

Still in a personal way the Emperor indicates the father of the querent, because it is from his father that his soul derives its elements. Some authors say this card means realization. That is correct so far as this word means an inner realizing of the significance of outer facts: the gathering of the harvest of experience, which will become the store of memory.

After I learned the first three numbers I was given to understand the Great Law of Four—the alpha and omega of all. I saw the Emperor on a lofty stone throne, ornamented by four rams' heads. On his forehead shone a golden helmet. His white beard fell over a purple mantle. In one hand he held a sphere, the symbol of his possession, and in the other, a scepter in the form of an Egyptian cross—the sign of his power over birth.

"I am The Great Law," the Emperor said. "I am the name of God. The four letters of his name are in me and I am in all. I am in the four principles. I am in the four elements. I am in the four seasons. I am in the four cardinal points. I am in the four signs of the Tarot. I am the beginning; I am action; I am completion; I am the result. For him who knows how to see me there are no mysteries on earth."

And while the Emperor spoke, his helmet shone brighter and brighter, and his golden armor gleamed beneath his mantle. I could not bear his glory and I lowered my eyes. When I tried to lift them again a vivid light of radiant fire was before me, and I prostrated myself and made obeisance to the Fiery Word.

Card V - The Hierophant

Divinatory Meanings: Marriage, alliance, captivity, servitude. Mercy and goodness, inspiration, a man to whom the Querent has recourse. Aspiration and breath. Sanction, holiness, religion.

Reversed: Society, good understanding, concord, over kindness, weakness.

The High Priest or *Hierophant, Spiritual Father, The Pope,* or *The Abbot* wears the triple crown and is seated between two pillars, but they are not those of the Temple which is guarded by the High Priestess, they are the pillars of Hermes and Solomon. The insignia of the figure is papal: in his left hand he holds a scepter terminating in the triple cross, and with his right hand he gives the well-known ecclesiastical sign which is called that of esotericism, distinguishing between the manifest and concealed part of doctrine (it is notable that the High Priestess makes no sign). The triple crown of the Hierophant and his triple crossed staff both indicate his rulership in the three worlds: the spiritual, the psychic, and the physical. At his feet are the crossed keys, and two priestly ministers in albs kneel before him. He has been usually called the Pope, which is a particular application of the more general office that he symbolizes—he is the ruling power of external religion.

He is the *summa totius theologiæ* (sum of all theology) when it has passed into the utmost rigidity of expression; but he symbolizes also all things that are righteous and sacred on the manifest side. As such, he is the channel of grace belonging to the world of institution as distinct from that of Nature, and the leader of salvation for the human race at large. He is the order and the head of the recognized hierarchy, which is the reflection of another and greater hierarchic order. He is not religion, although he is a mode of its expression. It may also be interpreted in its turn as the sanctifying of the profane (man) by the holy (man) in general.

Some say the card means marriage. This may be, but only in the inner sense of true revelation to the heart, and consequently in the same sense as Jesus meant when He said: "Marriages are contracted in Heaven." In practical divination, the card means *sanction*, be it of marriage or of something else, but always in the way of inner consent, not of outer law, which is ruled by another house. Self-centredness and some sort of natural authority are the chief characteristics of Leo and the Hierophant.

I saw the great Master in the Temple. Two initiates bowed before him and to them he spoke: "Seek the Path, do not seek attainment, seek for the Path within yourself. Do not expect to hear the truth from others, nor to see it, or read it in books. Look for the truth in yourself, not without yourself. Aspire only after the impossible and inaccessible. Expect only that which shall not be. Do not hope for Me, do not look for Me, do not believe—that I am outside yourself. Within your soul build a lofty tower by which you may ascend to Heaven. Do not believe in external miracles, expect miracles only within you. Beware of believing in a mystery of the earth, in a mystery guarded by men; for treasuries which must be guarded are empty.

"Do not search for a mystery that can be hidden by men. Seek the Mystery within yourself.

"Above all, avoid those towers built in order to preserve the mysteries and to make an ascent to Heaven by stone stairways. And remember that as soon as men build such a tower they begin to dispute about the summit. The Path is in yourself, and Truth is in yourself and Mystery is in yourself."

Card VI – The Lovers

Divinatory Meanings: Attraction, love, beauty, trials overcome. Health and sickness.

Reversed: Failure, foolish designs. A frustrated marriage and contrarieties of all kinds.

The sun shines in the zenith, and beneath is a great winged figure with arms extended, pouring down influences. In the foreground are a male and a female, unveiled before each other, as if Adam and Eve when they first occupied the paradise of the earthly body. Behind the man is the Tree of Life, bearing twelve fruits, and the Tree of the Knowledge of Good and Evil is behind the woman; the serpent is twining round it. The figures suggest youth, virginity, innocence, and love before it is contaminated by gross material desire. This is in all simplicity the card of human love, here exhibited as part of the way, the truth and the life.

The suggestion in respect of the woman is that she signifies that attraction towards the sensitive life which carries within it the idea of the Fall of Man, but she is rather the working of a Secret Law of Providence than a willing and conscious temptress. It is through her imputed lapse that man shall arise ultimately, and only by her can he complete himself. The card is therefore in its way another intimation concerning the great mystery of womanhood. The old meanings fall to pieces of necessity with the old pictures, but even as interpretations of the latter, some of them were of the order of commonplace and others were false in symbolism.

This symbol has undergone many variations, as might be expected from its subject. In the eighteenth century form, by which it first became known to the world of archaeological research, it is really a card of married life, showing father and mother, with their child placed between them; and the pagan Cupid above, in the act of flying his shaft, is, of course, a misapplied emblem. The Cupid is of love beginning rather than of love in its fullness, guarding the fruit thereof. The card is said to have been entitled *Simulacyum fidei*—the symbol of conjugal faith.

In the Marseilles Deck, between the Lovers, a beardless youth (the Magician, but also their child) is standing motionless in the angle where two roads meet. His arms form a diagonal cross upon his breast. The repetition of the 1st arcanum under another form. Here the man is not one of the Initiates. He does not know how to direct the magnetic currents of the Astral Light; he is therefore plunged in the antagonism of the different ideas which he cannot master. Two women, one on his right, the other on his left, each with one hand upon his shoulder, point to the two roads. The woman on the right has a circle of gold upon her head, the one on the left is disheveled and crowned with vine leaves. The future of the young man depends upon the road which he chooses.

In the garden I saw a Man and a Woman naked and beautiful. They loved each other and their Love was their service to the Great Conception; through It they communed with God, through It they received the highest revelations; in Its light the deepest truths came to them; the three kingdoms of nature, the mineral, plant and animal, and the four elements—fire, water, air and earth-served them.

Through their Love they saw the mystery of the world's equilibrium, and that they themselves were a symbol and expression of this balance. Two triangles united in them into a six-pointed star. Two magnets melted into an ellipsis. They were two. The third was the Unknown Future. The three made One.

Life is so good and the world so beautiful, and this man and woman wanted to believe in the reality of the world and of themselves. They wanted to forget service and take from the world what it can give. So they made a distinction between themselves and the world. They said, "We are here, the world is there," and the world separated from them and became hostile.

The everlasting mistake with men is that they see the fall in love. But Love is not a fall, it is a soaring above an abyss. And the higher the flight, the more beautiful and alluring appears the earth. But that wisdom, which crawls on earth, advises belief in the earth and in the present. This is the Temptation. And the man and woman yielded to it. They dropped from the eternal realms and submitted to time and death. The balance was disturbed. The fairyland was closed upon them. The Face of God ceased to reveal Itself to them, and all things appeared upside down.

Card VII – The Chariot

Divinatory Meanings: Aid in hardship, war, triumph, presumption, vengeance, trouble.

Reversed: Riot, quarrel, dispute, litigation, defeat.

The symbolism of this card corresponds in all points with the ideas which it expresses. A Conqueror, crowned with a coronet, upon which rise shining Pentagrams of gold, advances in a cubical chariot, surmounted by an azure, star-decked canopy supported by four columns. This symbol reproduces the 1st and 21st arcana in another order of ideas. The four columns represent the four animals of the 1st arcanum, and the four symbols of the 1st arcanum, symbols of the quaternary in all its acceptations.

The Conqueror, who occupies the centre of the four elements, is the man who has vanquished and directed the elementary forces: this victory is confirmed by the cubical form of the chariot, and by the Pentagrams, which crown the Initiate. The Conqueror has three right angles upon his cuirass, and he bears upon his shoulders the *Urim* and *Thummim* of the sovereign sacrificant, represented by the two crescents of the moon on the right and left; in his hand is a scepter.

Two sphinxes, one white, the other black, are harnessed to the chariot. The sphinxes are female entities, the driver of the Chariot is a man. This not only symbolizes the subjugation of Nature by will-power, but also the fact that, while inwardly "woman rules the world," rulership in the outer world lies with man, and it is his duty to keep within due bonds the forces of woman.

Upon the front of the cubical chariot, there is the Indian *lingam*, surmounted by the flying sphere of Egypt. The word *Yod-he-vau-he* is portrayed upon the front of the chariot by the winged globe, signifying the union of two principles. The two sphinxes correspond to the two principles, active and passive. The Conqueror corresponds especially with the Sword and the Vau of the sacred name.

He has led captivity captive; he is conquest on all planes—in the mind, in science, in progress, in certain trials of initiation. He has thus replied to the sphinx, and it is on this account that two sphinxes thus draw his chariot. He is above all things triumph in the mind.

It is to be understood that the planes of his conquest are external and not within himself, and the liberation which he effects may leave himself in the bondage of the logical understanding. If he came to the pillars of that Temple between which the High Priestess is seated, he could not open the scroll called Tora, nor if she questioned him could he answer.

In the eighteenth century white horses were yoked to the Chariot. As regards its usual name, the lesser stands for the greater; it is really the King in his triumph, typifying, however, the victory which creates kingship as its natural consequence and not the vested royalty. The Magician has become the Conqueror; the forces of good and of evil both drawing his chariot symbolize the fact that good and evil, agreeable as well as painful experiences, make us wiser and contain the elements of existence, spirit and matter both. The card may have to do with our adversaries.

This is Will armed with Knowledge. The man in the chariot thought himself a conqueror before he had really conquered, and he believes that victory must come to the conqueror. There are true possibilities in this beautiful conception, but also many false ones. This is indeed the Conqueror, but only for the moment; he has not yet conquered Time, and the succeeding moment is unknown to him. This is the Conqueror, not by love, but by fire and the sword, a conqueror against whom the conquered may arise. Behind him are the towers of the conquered city.

And he is unaware that the city vanquished by means of fire and the sword is the city within his own consciousness. He has externalized all these phases of his mind and sees them only outside himself. This is his fundamental error. He entered the outer court of the Temple of knowledge, but thinks he has been in the Temple itself. Because of this misconception great perils await him. He seeks to know and, perhaps, in order to attain, mistakes, dangers and even failures are necessary.

Understand that this is the same man whom you saw uniting Heaven and Earth, and again walking across a hot desert to a precipice.

Card VIII – Strength

Divinatory Meanings: Power, energy, action, courage, magnanimity. Complete success and honors.

Reversed: Despotism, abuse in power, weakness, discord, sometimes even disgrace.

A woman, over whose head there broods the same symbol of life which we have seen in the card of the Magician, is closing the jaws of a lion. The only point in which this design differs from the conventional presentations is that her beneficent fortitude has already subdued the lion, which is being led by a chain of flowers. The forces of nature, which we have mastered, are friendly to us and this is very well expressed by the woman who is closing the jaws of a lion. The latter stands for passion more particularly. She derives this force from the eternal or superhuman and this is indicated by the symbol of eternity above her head.

Early Renaissance must have seen this in the same way, as we find exactly the same image—only with one difference: it is there a young man, not a woman—a man closing the jaws of a lion in the capital of a pillar in the church of St. Andrew-the-Less in Vienna. It is, in fact, the image of the power given by the sacred science when justly applied.

The female figure is usually represented as closing the mouth of a lion. In the earlier form which is printed by Court de Gebelin, she is obviously opening it. The first alternative is better symbolically, but either is an instance of strength in its conventional understanding, and conveys the idea of mastery. It has been said that the figure represents organic force, moral force and the principle of all force.

The grappling on the card designates the hand of man in the act of grasping strongly. Ideas of strength are therefore applied to this card. It is the grip of friendship. A well-known symbol in many societies of brotherhood consists of two hands united in a close grip of friendship. We are united with that which we have mastered and with people who are able to respond to our emanations of thought, or to whose emanations we ourselves respond.

This is a picture of power, it has different meanings. First it shows the power of love. Love alone can conquer wrath. Hatred feeds hatred. Remember what Zarathustra said: "Let man be freed from vengeance; this is a bridge for me which leads to higher hope and a rainbow in heaven after long storms."

Then it shows power of unity. These wreaths of roses suggest a magic chain. Unity of desires, unity of aspirations creates such power that every wild, uncontrolled, unconscious force is subdued. Even two desires, if united, are able to conquer almost the whole world. The picture also shows the power of infinity, that sphere of mysteries.

Card IX – The Hermit

Divinatory Meanings: Treason, dissimulation, roguery, corruption. Prudence, consideration of all consequences.

Reversed: Concealment, disguise, policy, fear, unreasoned caution.

The Hermit is also *The Capuchin, Time,* and in more philosophical language *The Sage.* The variation from the conventional models in this card is only that the lamp is not enveloped partially in the mantle of its bearer, who blends the idea of the Ancient of Days with the Light of the World. It is a star which shines in the lantern. This is a card of attainment, rather than a card of quest; and to extend this conception the figure is seen holding up his beacon on an eminence. His beacon intimates that "where I am, you also may be." It refers to the truth that the Divine Mysteries secure their own protection from those who are unprepared.

It is as if a man who knows in his heart that all roads lead to the heights, and that God is at the great height of all, should choose the way of perdition or the way of folly as the path of his own attainment. The state of Royal Fortitude, which is the state of a Tower of Ivory and a House of Gold, but It is God and not the man who has become *Turris fortitudinis a facie inimici* (a tower of strength in the face of the enemy) and out of that House the enemy has been cast.

The corresponding counsel is that a man must not spare himself even in the presence of death, but he must be certain that his sacrifice shall be the best that will ensure his end. The axiom is that the strength which is raised to such a degree that a man dares lose himself shall learn how God is found. It is a doctrine of divine parsimony and conservation of energy, because of the stress, the terror and the manifest impertinences of this life.

The sign is that of thought-power, creative mind, idealism, which throw their own light on the things below, and consequently the Sagittarian is remarkable for always seeing things in his own light and trying to throw light on things in order to instruct other people. He is the eternal traveller, the indefatigable walker. And mentally he is always more or less lonely. All this is very distinctly symbolized in the card of the Hermit, which stands for ideas, perspectives, spiritual or moral influences and for light thrown upon the objects of this earth-life. In divination it stands for teachers, legal authorities, advisers and guides, and with the guiding principles in everything and questions, in relation to the querent. But above all it is his own idealism.

In the older cards the Hermit is shielding his light on one side with his mantle. This may be indicative of the habit of Sagittarians to evade and disarm contradiction beforehand, knowing by intuition the power of darkness. He is leaning on the staff of knowledge with regard to earthy matters.

The lantern of Hermes Trismegistus, this is higher knowledge, that inner knowledge which illuminates in a new way even what appears to be already clearly known. This lantern lights up the past, the present and the future for the Hermit, and opens the souls of people and the most intimate recesses. of their hearts. The cloak of Apollonius is the faculty of the wise man by which he isolates himself, even amidst a noisy crowd; it is his skill in hiding his mysteries, even while expressing them, his capacity for silence and his power to act in stillness. The staff of the patriarchs is his inner authority, his power, his self-confidence.

The lantern, the cloak and the staff are the three symbols of initiation. They are needed to guide souls past the temptation of illusory fires by the roadside, so that they may go straight to the higher goal. He who receives these three symbols or aspires to obtain them, strives to enrich himself with all he can acquire, not for himself, but, like God, to delight in the joy of giving.

Card X – Wheel of Fortune

Divinatory Meanings: Destiny, fortune, success, elevation, luck, felicity. Equilibrium, strength. The eternal action of time.

Reversed: Increase, abundance, an overly large amount.

The wheel has seven radii standing for the perpetual motion of a fluidic universe and for the flux of human life. Behind the general notion expressed in the symbol there lies the denial of chance and the fatality which is implied therein. The transliteration of Taro as Rota is inscribed on the wheel, counterchanged with the letters of the Divine Name—to show that Providence is present through all. But this is the Divine intention within, and the similar intention without is exemplified by the four Living Creatures.

The four Living Creatures of Ezekiel occupy the angles of the card. In the eighteenth century the ascending and descending animals were really of nondescript character, one of them having a human head. At the summit was another monster with the body of an indeterminate beast, wings on shoulders and a crown on head. It carried two wands in its claws. These are replaced in the reconstruction by a Hermanubis (Hermes and Aubis combined as one, the genius of good) ascending with the wheel, a Sphinx at the summit is the equilibrium of the wheel balancing good and evil with the sword in its lion claws, and Typhon (the Greek god of all the monsters, the genius of evil) in his serpent form is descending with the wheel.

The symbols of the four fixed signs are holding the four quarters of the card. The four fixed principles are indeed generally accepted as the basis of the material or concrete world. Compare the visions of Ezechiel and St. John of Patmos. The mid-heaven in the horoscope sees the eastern half of it rising and the western half on the other hand declining. See the right hand as the East and the left hand as the West, and you have the illustration of the horoscope more accurately still. As we know the East is standing for the source of spiritual force and inspiration, the West for the end of it and dying out.

It symbolizes Fortune, good or bad. So this means happenings, facts. It is the card of karma in the strict sense and that which is indicated by it in divination will come true or be realized actually. It is the point where you get at the world or the world gets at you. It is "ripe karma" above all, facts which are not to be overborne by words. The fruits of former thoughts.

I saw midway in the sky a huge, revolving circle covered with Kabalistic letters and symbols. The circle turned with terrible velocity, and around it, falling down and flying up, symbolic figures of the serpent and the dog revolved; above it sat an immovable sphinx. In clouds, on the four quarters of heaven, I saw the four apocalyptical beings, one with the face of a lion, another with the face of a bull, the third with a face of an eagle, and the fourth with the face of a bull. And each of them read an open book.

"Existence begins at every moment. The middle is everywhere. The way of eternity is a curve."

Card XI – Justice

Divinatory Meanings: Equity, rightness, honesty, integrity, executive. Triumph in law. Desire and achievement of things worked toward.

Reversed: Law in all its departments, legal complications, bigotry, bias, excessive severity.

Justice, or *Truth* portrayed as woman seen full face, and wearing an iron coronet, is seated upon a throne. She is placed between the two columns of the temple. The solar cross is traced upon her breast. The figure is seated between pillars, like the High Priestess, and on this account it seems to indicate the moral principle which deals unto every man according to his works differs in its essence from the spiritual justice which is involved in the idea of election. The latter belongs to a mysterious order of Providence, in virtue of which it is possible for certain men to conceive the idea of dedication to the highest things. The operation of this is like the breathing of the Spirit where it wills, and we have no canon of criticism or ground of explanation concerning it. In conclusion, the pillars of Justice open into one world and the pillars of the High Priestess into another.

The woman holds a balance in her left hand. The left hand *derives from*, while the right hand is instrumental in *giving out*. Scorpio derives from Libra the balance and the idea of justice, but the sword in the right hand shows, that we have not justice pure and simple, platonic so to speak, but that which has often been called avenging justice. The sword here is a sign of protection for the good, as well as a menace for the bad. Therefore, it is more vengeance than justice in every way and every form. It is the card of sorrow as well as of deeper satisfaction. In the man under this card there is always something of the avenger of wrongs, and very often it has to do with the proceedings of justice in the world.

Every mistake in the process of life will avenge itself with geometrical certainty. Continued effort results in the establishment of an equilibrium, between the destruction of the works of man accomplished by nature, when left to herself, and the preservation of this work. Hence the idea of balancing power, and consequently of Justice attributed to this letter. This house is the school of life and in this house the Self takes from life and from the cosmos surrounding what it wants, consequently what it does not yet possess, and the card of Justice becomes the index for our debts or the possessions of other people.

So the card of Justice additionally indicates the faculty of desire, higher as well as lower, from the most spiritual or religious longing down to the most crude lust. Sexual experience is one of the most important expressions of it, and we may safely say, that one of the principal significances of the card is sex. Another, principally where sex is sublimated, is occult experience, and the psychical side of earth-life in general.

The female figure is said to be Astræa, who personified the same virtue and is represented by the same symbols. This goddess notwithstanding, and notwithstanding the vulgarian Cupid, the Tarot is not of Roman mythology, or of Greek either. Its presentation of justice is supposed to be one of the four cardinal virtues included in the sequence of Greater Arcana; but, as it so happens, the fourth emblem is wanting, and it became necessary for the commentators to discover it at all costs.

When I possessed the keys, read the book and understood the symbols, I was permitted to lift the curtain of the Temple and enter its inner sanctum. And there I beheld a Woman with a crown of gold and a purple mantle. She held a sword in one hand and scales in the other. I trembled with awe at her appearance, which was deep and mysterious, and drew me like an abyss.

"You see Truth. On these scales everything is weighed. This sword is always raised to guard justice, and nothing can escape it. But why do you avert your eyes from the scales and the sword? They will remove the last illusions. How could you live on earth without these illusions? You wished to see Truth and now you behold it! But remember what happens to the mortal who beholds a Goddess!"

Card XII – The Hanged Man

Divinatory Meanings: Wisdom, seeing all possibilities, knowledge of the divine, trials, sacrifice, intuition, divination, prophecy. Knowledge that ultimately injures the hearer.

Reversed: Selfishness, the crowd, the nation.

A man hanging by one foot to a gibbet, resting upon two trees, each bearing six branches, which have been cut off. The man's hands are tied behind his back, and the fold of his arms forms the base of a reversed triangle, of which his head forms the point. His eyes are open and his fair hair floats upon the wind. His right leg crosses his left and so forms a cross. The man is shown hanging in a sling on one foot. Astrology teaches that the feet are ruled by the sign Pisces. The crossing of the legs is a symbol of *crossing* in general.

The gallows from which he is suspended forms a Tau cross, while the figure—from the position of the legs—forms a hooked cross (a swastika). There is a nimbus around his head in the style of a martyr. It should be noted (1) that the tree of sacrifice is living wood, with leaves thereon; (2) that the face expresses deep entrancement, not suffering; (3) that the figure, as a whole, suggests life in suspension.

It is a card of profound significance, but all the significance is veiled. Like the sun placed in the midst of the signs of the Zodiac (six signs on each side represented by the lopped branches), our young hero is suspended between two decisions, from which will spring his spiritual future. This Hanged Man serves for an example to the presumptuous, and his position indicates discipline, the absolute submission which the human owes to the Divine. Divine expansion in humanity is produced by the prophets and revelation, and this inspires the idea of the revealed law. But the revelation of the law involves punishment for him who violates it, or elevation for him who understands it; and here we find the ideas of punishment, of violent death, voluntary or involuntary.

Astrologically, the card indicates things which we have not yet mastered and those whom we have failed to understand or who have failed to understand us. In the eyes of the world it is the sign of waste, spoil, mishap. Viewed from the other side, the outer world loses its importance or even reality, and the consciousness is opened to inner truth.

This is the reversing of consciousness, which makes things change their significance in such a way that they appear to turn upside down: the world is now viewed from the other side. And this is the significance of the hanged man.

Look! This is a man who saw Truth. Suffering awaits the man on earth, who finds the way to eternity and to the understanding of the Endless. He is still a man, but he already knows much of what is inaccessible even to Gods. And the incommensurableness of the small and the great in his soul constitutes his pain and his golgotha. In his own soul appears the gallows on which he hangs in suffering, feeling that he is indeed inverted. He chose this way himself. For this he went over a long road from trial to trial, from initiation to initiation, through failures and falls. And now he has found Truth and knows himself.

He knows that it is he who stands before an altar with magic symbols, and reaches from earth to heaven; that he also walks on a dusty road under a scorching sun to a precipice where a crocodile awaits him; that he dwells with his mate in paradise under the shadow of a blessing genius; that he is chained to a black cube under the shadow of deceit; that he stands as a victor for a moment in an illusionary chariot drawn by sphinxes; and that with a lantern in bright sunshine, he seeks for Truth in a desert. Now he has found Her.

Card XIII – Death

Divinatory Meanings: End, mortality, destruction, corruption. The failure of marriage projects. Rebirth, creation, renewal.

Reversed: Inertia, sleep, lethargy, petrifaction. Hope destroyed.

The mysterious horseman moves slowly, bearing a black banner emblazoned with the Mystic Rose, which signifies life. Between two pillars on the verge of the horizon there shines the sun of immortality. The horseman carries no visible weapon, but king and child and maiden fall before him, while a prelate with clasped hands awaits his end.

The picture speaks for itself, but still there is more in it than we might suppose at first sight. Beyond all doubt it is a sort of allegorical representation of Father Chronos, who, while creating, consumes his own children, and was very often pictured as a warning of death or a remembrance of mortality. But on the other hand Time marks the beginning, and birth is not less under his government than death. The earlier editions of this card show the figure harvesting heads and limbs of human bodies upon a field. This may be an expression of an old superstition, which said that those limbs with which man sinned would grow out of his grave.

Creation necessitates equal destruction in a contrary sense, and therefore all the regenerations that have sprung from previous destruction, all transformations, and consequently death, are regarded as the passage from one world to the other. The ideas expressed by this arcanum are those of destruction preceding or following regeneration. The thirteenth card of the Tarot is placed between the invisible and the visible worlds. It is the universal link in nature, the means by which all the influences react from one world to the other.

The natural transit of man to the next stage of his being either is or may be one form of his progress, but the exotic and almost unknown entrance, while still in this life, into the state of mystical death is a change in the form of consciousness and the passage into a state to which ordinary death is neither the path nor gate. In the exotic sense it has been said to signify the ascent of the spirit in the divine spheres, creation and destruction, perpetual movement, and so forth. The transparent and unescapable meaning is death, but the alternatives allocated to the symbol are change and transformation.

The hieroglyphic meaning of the Mem (13th letter of the Hebrew alphabet) is a woman, the companion of man, it therefore gives rise to ideas of fertility and formation.

I saw a gigantic rider on a white horse, dressed in black armor, with a black helmet and black plume. A skeleton's face looked out from under the helmet. One bony hand held a large, black, slowly-waving banner, and the other held a black bridle ornamented with skulls and bones. And, wherever the white horse passed, night and death followed; flowers withered, leaves drooped, the earth covered itself with a white shroud; graveyards appeared; towers, castles and cities were destroyed.

Kings in the full splendor of their fame and their power; beautiful women loved and loving; high priests invested by power from God; innocent children—when they saw the white horse all fell on their knees before him, stretched out their hands in terror and despair, and fell down to rise no more.

Afar, behind two towers, the sun sank. A deadly cold enveloped me. The heavy hoofs of the horse seemed to step on my breast, and I felt the world sink into an abyss. But all at once something familiar, but faintly seen and heard, seemed to come from the measured step of the horse. A moment more and I heard in his steps the movement of the Wheel of Life!

An illumination entered me, and, looking at the receding rider and the descending sun, I understood that the Path of Life consists of the steps of the horse of Death. "Yes," said the voice. "The sun does not think of its going down and coming up. What does it know of earth, of the going and coming observed by men? It goes its own way, over its own orbit, round an unknown Centre. Life, death, rising and falling—do you not know that all these things are thoughts and dreams and fears of the Fool?"

Card XIV – Temperance

Divinatory Meanings: Economy, moderation, frugality, management accommodation.

Reversed: Things connected with churches, religions, sects, the priesthood Disunion, unfortunate combinations, competing interests.

A winged angel, with the sign of the sun upon its forehead and on its breast the square and triangle of the septenary. The square with inscribed triangle reminds us of the passage of the cosmological Stanzas of Dzyan, "The Three fall into the Four," which means the beginning of Manifestation. The figure is neither male nor female. It is held to be pouring the essences of life from one chalice to another chalice. It has one foot upon the earth and one upon waters, thus illustrating the nature of the essences. A direct path goes up to certain heights on the verge of the horizon, and above there is a great light through which a crown is seen vaguely. Hereof is some part of the Secret of Eternal Life as it is possible to man in his incarnation. All the conventional emblems are renounced herein.

So also are the conventional meanings, which refer to changes in the seasons perpetual movement of life and even the combination of ideas. It is called Temperance fantastically, because, when the rule of it arrives in our consciousness, it tempers combines and harmonizes the psychic and material natures. Under that rule we know in our rational part something of whence we came and whither we are going. The name Temperance appears to have been chosen because of the transposition from one plane to another, or one centre to another, which has much to do with time also.

The upper vase and the lower one illustrate this distribution from higher to lower regions. So this card signifies all sorts of distribution, from the nervous system and its workings of co-ordination to correspondence by the post office, letters and communications, and the latter not only limited to this physical world but extended to other planes of existence.

An angel in a white robe, touching earth and heaven, appeared. His wings were flame and a radiance of gold was about his head. On his breast he wore the sacred sign of the book of the Tarot—a triangle within a square, a point within the triangle; on his forehead the symbol of life and eternity, the circle. In one hand was a cup of silver, in the other a cup of gold and there flowed between these cups a constant, glistening stream of every color of the rainbow. But I could not tell from which cup nor into which cup the stream flowed.

The name of the angel is Time. The circle on his forehead is the symbol of eternity and life. Each life is a circle which returns to the same point where it began. Death is the return to birth. And from one point to another on the circumference of a circle the distance is always the same, and the further it is from one point, the nearer it will be to the other.

One of the cups the angel holds is the past, the other is the future. The rainbow stream between the cups is the present. You see that it flows both ways. This is Time in its most incomprehensible aspect. Men think that all flows constantly in one direction. They do not see that everything perpetually meets and that Time is a multitude of turning circles. Understand this mystery and learn to discern the contrary currents in the rainbow stream of the present. The symbol of the sacred book of the Tarot on the angel's breast is the symbol of the correlation of God, Man and the Universe.

Card XV – The Devil

Divinatory Meanings: Ravage, violence, vehemence, extraordinary efforts or energy, force, fatality. That which is predestined, but not necessarily evil. Sexual problems.

Reversed: Evil fatality, weakness, pettiness, blindness.

The Horned Goat of Mendes, with wings like those of a bat, is standing on an altar. At the pit of the stomach there is the sign of Mercury. The right hand is upraised and extended, being the reverse of that benediction which is given by the Hierophant in the fifth card. In the left hand there is a great flaming torch, inverted towards the earth. A reversed pentagram is on the forehead. There is a ring in front of the altar, from which two chains are carried to the necks of two figures, male and female. These are analogous with those of The Lovers, as if Adam and Eve after the Fall. Here, the chain is of fatality and of the material life. The figures are tailed, to signify the animal nature, but there is human intelligence in the faces, and he who is exalted above them is not to be their master for ever. Even now, he is also a bondsman, sustained by the evil that is in him and blind to the liberty of service.

In the eighteenth century this card seems to have been rather a symbol of merely animal impudicity. Except for a fantastic head-dress, the chief figure is entirely naked; it has bat-like wings, and the hands and feet are represented by the claws of a bird. In the right hand there is a scepter terminating in a sign which has been thought to represent fire.

Since 1856 the influence of Éliphas Lévi and his doctrine of occultism has changed the face of this card, and it now appears as a Baphometic figure with the head of a goat and a great torch between the horns; it is seated instead of erect, and in place of the generative organs there is the Hermetic caduceus. In *Le Tarot Divinatoire* of Papus the small demons are replaced by naked human beings, male and female who are yoked only to each other.

The goat-like figure recalls the sign Capricorn in which astrology teaches that the planet Mars has its exaltation, the name Devil means evil and this alliteration holds good not only in English. Allusion to sex-problems is found in the two human figures, man and woman, chained to the pedestal on which the diabolic figure is seated. That sex-nature binds man, is a natural fact of a more or less occult order. So it has to do with generation in Nature in every sense and kingdom, though astrology teaches that Mars has a special connection with the animal kingdom and animal passion—passion which drives to the preservation of the body as well as of the race; fighting for existence in both senses of the term. The torch in the hand of the figure denotes, of course, the fire of passion and desire, which may rise to anger and rage. So it may well be said to represent the condition of the struggle for existence.

But a little attentive consideration of the symbol will show us that it contains several of the details which we have already seen in other figures of the Tarot, but under a different aspect.

If we place the Juggler by the side of the Devil we shall see that the arms of the two personages are using the same gesture, but in an inverse sense. The Juggler points his right hand towards the Universe, his left hand towards God; on the other hand the Devil raises his right hand into the air, while his left points to the earth. Instead of the magic-initiating wand of the Juggler, the Demon holds the lighted torch, the symbol of black magic and of destruction.

By the side of the Devil, and balanced by him, are two personages reproducing the same symbolism that we find in the Lovers, and in the two supports of the gibbet of the Hanged Man. The universal vivifying force represented by the 3rd arcanum, has here become the universal destroying force. The scepter of Venus-Urania has become the Demon's torch, the Angel's wings have changed into the hideous pinions.

Black, awful night enveloped the earth. An ominous, red flame burned in the distance. I was approaching a fantastic figure which outlined itself before me as I came nearer to it. High above the earth appeared the repulsive red face of the Devil, with large, hairy ears, pointed beard and curved goats' horns. A pentagram, pointing downwards, shone in phosphoric light between the horns on his forehead. Two large, grey, bat-like wings were spread behind him. He held up one arm, spreading out his bare, fat hand. In the palm I saw the sign of black magic. A burning torch held down-end in his other hand emitted black, stifling smoke.

A man and woman were chained to the cube—the same Man and Woman I saw in the garden, but now they had horns and tails tipped with flame. And they were evidently dissatisfied in spirit, and were filled with protest and repulsion. This is a picture of weakness. A picture of falsehood and evil. They are the same man and woman you saw in the garden, but their love ceasing to be a sacrifice, became an illusion.

This man and woman forgot that their love is a link in the chain that unites them with eternity, that their love is a symbol of equilibrium and a road to Infinity. They forgot that It is a key to the gate of the magic world, the torch which lights the higher Path. They forgot that Love is real and immortal and they subjugated it to the unreal and temporary. And they each made love a tool for submitting the other to himself. Then love became dissension and fettered them with iron chains to the black cube of matter, on which sits deceit.

And I heard the voice of the Devil: "I am Evil," he said, "In order to see me, one must be able to see unfairly, incorrectly and narrowly. I close the triangle, the other two sides of which are Death and Time. In order to quit this triangle it is necessary to see that it does not exist."

Card XVI – The Tower

Divinatory Meanings: Misery, distress, indigence, adversity, calamity, disgrace, deception, ruin. Unforeseen catastrophe.

Reversed: The same in a lesser degree. Oppression, imprisonment, tyranny.

The Tower, Castle of Plutus, God's House and *The Tower of Babel* bears the picture of a tower, with its battlements struck by lightning; two men, one crowned, the other uncrowned, are falling with the fragments of broken masonry; the attitude of the former recalls the shape of the Hebrew letter, Ayin. Ayin is addicted to this card. It expresses all that is crooked, false, perverse, and bad.

There is a sense in which the catastrophe is a reflection from the previous card, but not on the side of the symbolism which I have tried to indicate therein. It is more correctly a question of analogy; one is concerned with the fall into the material and animal state, while the other signifies destruction on the intellectual side. The Tower has been spoken of as the chastisement of pride and the intellect overwhelmed in the attempt to penetrate the Mystery of God; but in neither case do these explanations account for the two persons who are the living sufferers. The one is the literal word made void and the other its false interpretation. In yet a deeper sense, it may signify also the end of a dispensation, but there is no possibility here for the consideration of this involved question.

The figures falling from the Tower are held to be Nimrod and his minister. It is assuredly a card of confusion. The lightning would symbolize the fire and sword with which that edifice was visited by the King of the Chaldees. Alternatively, the stone tower struck by a flash of lightning is a version of the legend of Ouranos mutilating his son Chronos, which means, that Heaven is not content with a body of fixed dimensions and form, nor any heavenly force with the limitations put to it by physical authorities or architects. This may warn man, not to build upon physical existence alone or to think himself safe upon a material basis, however high and solid it may appear from a material point of view.

So the card of the Tower signifies the relation between macro- and micro-cosm and will mean rupture, sudden disillusion, disenchantment, but also it symbolizes intuition, renewal, help from above and clear insight in relation to vanity and sham projects, illusion and meaningless formalism.

I saw a lofty tower extending from earth to heaven; its golden crowned summit reached beyond the clouds. All round it black night reigned and thunder rumbled. Suddenly the heavens opened, a thunder-clap shook the whole earth, and lightning struck the summit of the tower and felled the golden crown. A tongue of fire shot from heaven and the whole tower became filled with fire and smoke. Then I beheld the builders of the tower fall headlong to the ground.

The building of the tower was begun by the disciples of the great Master in order to have a constant reminder of the Master's teaching that the true tower must be built in one's own soul, that in the tower built by hands there can be no mysteries, that no one can ascend to Heaven by treading stone steps. The tower should warn the people not to believe in it. It should serve as a reminder of the inner Temple and as a protection against the outer; it should be as a lighthouse, in a dangerous place where men have often been wrecked and where ships should not go.

But by and by the disciples forgot the true covenant of the Master and what the tower symbolized, and began to believe in the tower of stone, they had built, and to teach others to so believe. They began to say that in this tower there is power, mystery and the spirit of the Master, that the tower itself is holy and that it is built for the coming Master according to His covenant and His will. And so they waited in the tower for the Master. Others did not believe this, or interpreted it differently. They had begun to think that this is the tower of the Master, that He builds it through them, and that it must and, indeed, can be built right up to Heaven.

And you see how Heaven responded?

Card XVII – The Star

Divinatory Meanings: Benefit, well-doing, organization, love, beauty, peace. Loss or privation.

Reversed: Arrogance, haughtiness, impotence. Laziness, weakness.

The Star, *Dog-Star*, *Sirius*, or the *Star of the Magi* is a great, radiant star of eight rays, surrounded by seven lesser stars—also of eight rays. The eight stars correlate with the eight planets of the solar system. The female figure in the foreground is entirely naked. Her left knee is on the land and her right foot upon the water. She pours Water of Life from two great cups, irrigating sea and land.

Behind her is rising ground and on the right, a bird (an ibis, sacred to the Egyptians as the god Toth) is perched on a tree near her (a butterfly on a rose has been substituted in some later cards). Here we find the symbol of immortality. The soul (ibis or butterfly) will survive the body, which is only a place of trial (the ephemeral flower). The courage to bear these trials will come from above (the stars).

The figure expresses eternal youth and beauty. That which the figure communicates to the living scene is the substance of the heavens and the elements. No astrologer will hesitate to recognize Venus. The picture on the card shows it quite clearly: a naked girl, demonstrating undoubtedly the beauty of the human body, symbol of beauty in the nature of man. Well, then it is the image of this planet of beauty and eternal youth, which has its place between the Sun and Mercury on one side and our Earth on the other, the third personification of the genius of the Sun. The ibis and the butterfly connect the idea of immortality with this figure, in perfect accord with the mystic teaching which says, that love extends beyond the grave.

For the majority of prepared minds, the figure will appear as the type of Truth unveiled, glorious in undying beauty, pouring on the waters of the soul some part and measure of her priceless possession. But she is in reality the Great Mother in the Kabalistic *Sephira Binah*, which is supernal Understanding, who communicates through the Sephirot—the ten emanations in Kabbalah through which *Ein Sof* (The Infinite) reveals himself and continuously creates both the physical realm and the chain of higher metaphysical realms that are below in the measure that they can receive her influx.

And beneath the radiant stars beside the blue river I saw a naked maiden, young and beautiful. She stooped on one knee and poured water from two vessels, one of gold and one of silver. A little bird in a near by bush lifted its wings and was poised ready to fly away. For a moment I understood that I beheld the Soul of Nature.

This is Nature's Imagination. Nature dreams, improvises, creates worlds. Learn to unite your imagination with Her Imagination and nothing will ever be impossible for you. Lose the external world and seek it in yourself. Then you will find Light. But remember, unless you have lost the Earth, you will not find Heaven. It is impossible to see both wrongly and rightly at the same time.

Card XVIII – The Moon

Divinatory Meanings: Hidden enemies, danger, uncertainty, darkness, terror, deception, error. Dreams, exhibitions, games, theaters, the lower class of people. Unhelpful people.

Reversed: Instability, inconstancy, silence, lesser degrees of deception and error.

A meadow feebly lighted by the moon. The light, the symbol of the soul, no longer reaches us directly; the material world is only lighted by reflection. The meadow is bounded by a tower on each side. Drops of blood are falling from the moon. The material world is the last point which the spirit can reach, it can descend no lower; this is shown by the boundaries of the field. The drops of blood represent the descent of the Spirit into Matter. A path sprinkled with drops of blood loses itself in the horizon. In the centre of the field a dog and a wolf axe howling at the moon, a crayfish is climbing out of the water between the two animals.

The distinction between this card and some of the conventional types is that the moon is increasing on what is called the side of mercy, to the right of the observer. It has sixteen chief and sixteen secondary rays. The card represents life of the imagination apart from life of the spirit. The path between the towers is the issue into the unknown. The dog and wolf are the fears of the natural mind in the presence of that place of exit, when there is only reflected light to guide it. Servile spirits (the dog), savage souls (the wolf), and crawling creatures (the crayfish) are all present watching the fall of the soul, hoping to aid in its destruction. And it may happen to us, that a lower current of the Moon brings our way people who have no higher aim than to aid in our destruction even if we ourselves have no intention whatever of falling.

The last reference is a key to another form of symbolism. The intellectual light is a reflection and beyond it is the unknown mystery which it cannot show forth. It illuminates our animal nature, types of which are represented below—the dog, the wolf and that which comes up out of the deeps, the nameless and hideous tendency which is lower than the savage beast. It strives to attain manifestation, symbolized by crawling from the abyss of water to the land, but as a rule it sinks back whence it came. The face of the mind directs a calm gaze upon the unrest below; the dew of thought falls; the message is: Peace, be still; and it may be that there shall come a calm upon the animal nature, while the abyss beneath shall cease from giving up a form.

This card consequently means the life of the soul in particular, the feelings and sentiments, emotions, changes wrought in existence by them, water and the female element in general. In the horoscopic figure it may be the mother or some other woman prominent in the life of the querent; it may signify women in general. It is the sign of *panta rei*: everything passing, flowing or ebbing away in life, consequently uncertainty.

A desolate plain stretched before me. A full moon looked down as if in contemplative hesitation. Under her wavering light the shadows lived their own peculiar life. On the horizon I saw blue hills, and over them wound a path which stretched between two grey towers far away into the distance. On either side the path a wolf and dog sat and howled at the moon. I remembered that dogs believe in thieves and ghosts. A large black crab crawled out of the rivulet into the sands. A heavy, cold dew was falling.

Dread fell upon me. I sensed the presence of a mysterious world, a world of hostile spirits, of corpses rising from graves, of wailing ghosts. In this pale moonlight I seemed to feel the presence of apparitions; someone watched me from behind the towers, and I knew it was dangerous to look back.

Card XIX – The Sun

Divinatory Meanings: Material happiness, fortunate marriage, contentment.
Reversed: The same in a lesser sense.

The naked child mounted on a white horse and displaying a red standard has been mentioned already as the better symbolism connected with this card. It is the destiny of the Supernatural East and the great and holy light which goes before the endless procession of humanity, coming out from the walled garden of the sensitive life and passing on the journey home. The card signifies, therefore, the transit from the manifest light of this world, represented by the glorious sun of earth, to the light of the world to come, which goes before aspiration and is typified by the heart of a child.

But the last allusion is again the key to a different form or aspect of the symbolism. The sun is that of consciousness in the spirit: the direct as the antithesis of the reflected light. The characteristic type of humanity has become a little child therein—a child in the sense of simplicity and innocence in the sense of wisdom. In that simplicity, he bears the seal of Nature and of Art; in that innocence, he signifies the restored world. When the self-knowing spirit has dawned in the consciousness above the natural mind, that mind in its renewal leads forth the animal nature in a state of perfect conformity.

The luminary is distinguished in older cards by chief rays that are waved and salient alternately and by secondary salient rays. It appears to shed its influence on earth not only by light and heat, but—like the moon—by drops of dew. Court de Gebelin termed these tears of gold and of pearl, just as he identified the lunar dew with the tears of Isis. Beneath the dog-star there is a wall suggesting an enclosure-as it might be, a walled garden-wherein are two children, either naked or lightly clothed, facing a water, and gamboling, or running hand in hand.

"The walls indicate that we are still in the visible or material world. The two children symbolize the two creative fluids, positive and negative, of the new creature." This relates to the picture which shows a child on horseback—or two children as in the older editions of the card—playing beneath the bright Sun and evidently within a walled enclosure. So far so good: we are and we remain in this world. And for the rest the Sun is the Sun and this card means everything that astrology can tell about the Sun, in every respect and on all planes. It means the positive or masculine elements in general, the power and function of will and concentration, great benefit and mighty protection in spiritual as well as in mundane life and matters. It may signify the father of the querent and high authorities, king, president, or a ruler. The spiritual centre of man and the centre of importance in everything is indicated by it.

As soon as I perceived the Sun, I understood that It, Itself, is the expression of the Fiery Word and the sign of the Emperor. The great luminary shone with an intense heat upon the large golden heads of sun-flowers. And I saw a naked boy, whose head was wreathed with roses, galloping on a white horse and waving a bright-red banner.

I shut my eyes for a moment and when I opened them again I saw that each ray of the Sun is the scepter of the Emperor and bears life. And I saw how under the concentration of these rays the mystic flowers of the waters open and receive the rays into themselves and how all Nature is constantly born from the union of two principles.

Card XX – Judgement

Divinatory Meanings: Change of position, renewal. Illumination, vain aspirations. Ideals.

Reversed: Weakness, pusillanimity, simplicity. Deliberation, decision, sentence.

The great angel is here encompassed by clouds, but he blows his bannered trumpet, and the cross as usual is displayed on the banner. The dead are rising from their tombs—a woman on the right, a man on the left hand, and between them their child, whose back is turned. But in this card there are more than three who are restored, and it has been thought worth while to make this variation as illustrating the insufficiency of current explanations. It should be noted that all the figures are as one in the wonder, adoration and ecstasy expressed by their attitudes. It is the card which registers the accomplishment of the great work of transformation in answer to the summons of the Supernal—which summons is heard and answered from within.

Herein is the intimation of a significance which cannot well be carried further in the present place. What is that within us which does sound a trumpet and all that is lower in our nature rises in response—almost in a moment, almost in the twinkling of an eye? Let the card continue to depict, for those who can see no further, the Last judgment and the resurrection in the natural body; but let those who have inward eyes look and discover therewith. They will understand that it has been called truly in the past a card of eternal life, and for this reason it may be compared with that which passes under the name of Temperance.

Before rejecting the transparent interpretation of the symbolism which is conveyed by the name of the card and by the picture which it presents to the eye, we should feel very sure of our ground. On the surface, at least, it is and can be only the resurrection of that triad—father, mother, child—whom we have met with already in the eighth card. Others say that it signifies renewal, which is obvious enough; that it is the triad of human life; that it is the "generative force of the earth ... and eternal life."

So this card may stand for ideals, religious, social or any other and for the elevating effect they have on man; for ideas and leading motives, aspirations. Consequently for generalization, illumination, dispersion, elevation, for all that is honorable on one hand, but also for illusions or vain aspirations on the other hand. It is the sign of deliverance from narrow thought and hampering conditions in the soul as well as in the body and in life.

I saw an ice plain, and on the horizon, a chain of snowy mountains. A cloud appeared and began to grow until it covered a quarter of the sky. Two fiery wings suddenly expanded in the cloud, and I knew that I beheld the messenger of the Empress. He raised a trumpet and blew through it vibrant, powerful tones. The plain quivered in response to him and the mountains loudly rolled their echoes. One after another, graves opened in the plain and out of them came men and women, old and young, and children. They stretched out their arms toward the Messenger of the Empress and to catch the sounds of his trumpet.

And in its tones I felt the smile of the Empress and in the opening graves I saw the opening flowers whose fragrance seemed to be wafted by the outstretched arms. Then I understood the mystery of birth in death.

Card XXI – The World

Divinatory Meanings: Assured success, recompense, voyage, route, flight, change of place.

Reversed: Inertia, fixity, stagnation, permanence.

At the four angles of the card we find the four animals of the Apocalypse, and the four forms of the Sphinx: the Man, the Lion, the Bull, and the Eagle grouped about an elliptic garland, as if it were a chain of flowers intended to symbolize all sensible things. The garland is a symbol of humanity and the eternal reward of a life that has been spent well.

Within this garland there is the figure of a woman, whom the wind has girt about the loins with a light scarf, and this is all her vesture. She holds her legs in the same cross as the Hanged Man, and carries a wand in either hand. It is eloquent as an image of the swirl of the sensitive life, of joy attained in the body, of the soul's intoxication in the earthly paradise, but still guarded by the Divine Watchers, as if by the powers and the graces of the Holy Name, Tetragammaton, JVHV—those four ineffable letters which are sometimes attributed to the mystical beasts. The symbols of the four fixed signs are presented at the corners of the cards, and where these fixed signs are seen as the foundation stones of our physical world.

Appropriated to the world of men, it must mean that which falls outside our will-power, cosmic conditions to which we are subject, but which at the f same time provide us with all that is wanted for our physical conditions. The latter of course became the reason for attaching to this card a generally beneficial influence, especially in the domain of the senses. It means that if we row with the cosmic tide, we shall enjoy happiness and everything we want, but on the other hand we must not neglect the implicit possibility, that when rowing against the tidal current of the world, we shall experience trouble and no end of it, or if we 'cross the stream' we shall have to stand firm on our legs. So besides the joy of the senses, this card means also the cosmic origin of life, to which the candidate for initiation returns, and which now and then appears in dreams.

The World must have had a larger meaning, originally, than that of the world of beings moving on the surface of our Earth, and the oval figure may well have stood for the form of the solar system at large, with its planets moving in oval orbs.

As this final message of the Major Trumps represents also the perfection and end of the Cosmos, the secret which is within it, the rapture of the universe when it understands itself in God. It is further the state of the soul in the consciousness of Divine Vision, reflected from the self-knowing spirit. It has more than one message on the macrocosmic side and is, for example, the state of the restored world when the law of manifestation shall have been carried to the highest degree of natural perfection. But it is perhaps more especially a story of the past, referring to that day when all was declared to be good, when the morning stars sang together and all the Sons of God shouted for joy.

An unexpected vision appeared to me. A circle not unlike a wreath woven from rainbow and lightnings, whirled from heaven to earth with a stupendous, velocity, blinding me by its brilliance. And amidst this light and fire I heard music and soft singing, thunderclaps and the roar of a tempest, the rumble of falling mountains and earthquakes. The circle whirled with a terrifying noise, touching the sun and the earth, and, in the centre of it I saw the naked, dancing figure of a beautiful young woman, enveloped by a light, transparent scarf, in her hand she held a magic wand.

Presently the four apocalyptical beasts began to appear on the edges of the circle; one with the face of a lion, another with the face of a man, the third, of an eagle and the fourth, of a bull.

The vision disappeared as suddenly as it appeared. A weird silence fell on me. "What does it mean," I asked in wonder.

A voice said, "It is the image of the world, but it can be understood only after the Temple has been entered. This is a vision of the world in the circle of Time, amidst the four principles. But thou seest differently because thou seest the world outside thyself. Learn to see it in thyself and thou wilt understand the infinite essence, hidden in all illusory forms."

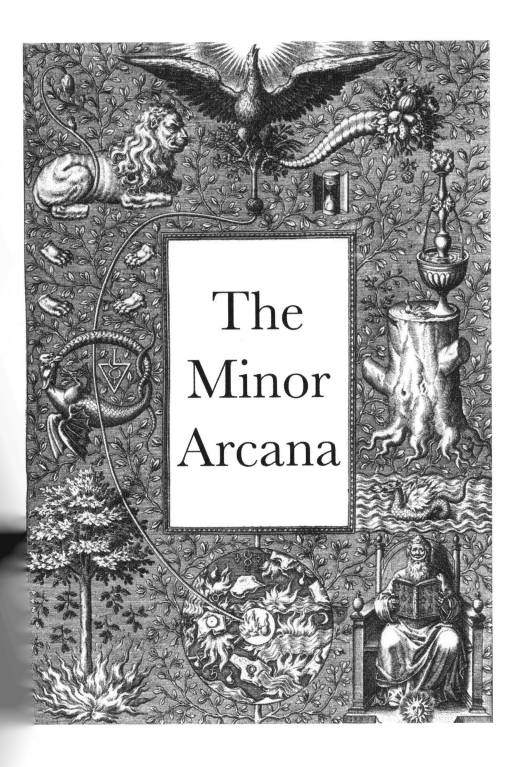

The Minor Arcana

King of Wands

Divinatory Meanings: Dark man, friendly, countryman, generally married, honest and conscientious. Honesty. News concerning an unexpected heritage. A good marriage.
Reversed: Good, but severe; austere, yet tolerant. Advice that should be followed.

The physical and emotional nature to which this card is attributed is dark, ardent, lithe, animated, impassioned, noble. The King uplifts a flowering wand, and wears, like his three correspondences in the remaining suits, what is called a cap of maintenance beneath his crown. He connects with the symbol of the lion, which is emblazoned on the back of his throne. Country gentleman, man with good intentions and yet severe, honest and conscientious; may be a peasant or agriculturist.

Higher octave of the ace, lord of the suit of Air and the mind; coming on the First house. What may have led to the legend of calling him a country gentleman and bringing the whole suit of wands more or less in relation with the country, is not clear. He is the lord of the intellectual kingdom, consequently he may denote every authority or personality of primary importance in some or other intellectual, mercurial or mercenary line. It must be some one representing a high authority himself or uniting opposite interests, while he himself, on account of the same authority he represents, may not or cannot be contradicted.

A governor, director of business, high official, postmaster, solicitor, manager, independent trader, Secretary of State, and the principles or functions for which they stand. The house of Mars imparts austerity, security and generally initiative and honesty; in weak cases there may be, however, some doubt with regard to his absolute integrity.

Queen of Wands

Divinatory Meanings: A dark woman, countrywoman, friendly, chaste, loving, honorable. If the card beside her signifies a man, she is well disposed towards him; if a woman, she is interested in the Querent. Also, love of money, or a certain success in business. A good harvest.

Reversed: Good, economical, obliging, serviceable. Goodwill towards the Querent, but without the opportunity to exercise it.

The Wands throughout this suit are always in leaf, as it is a suit of life and animation. Emotionally and otherwise, the Queen's personality corresponds to that of the King, but is more magnetic. Country woman, honest, economical woman, honorable and loving, virtuous, chaste, good and inclined to be friendly and interest herself in the querent. The card may also indicate love of money, economy and gifts.

Queen of Air on the Second house of economy, money, country life and art. Some of the traditional renderings certify this remarkably well. Now what does a queen in general mean? In divination a woman simply, but in general, as the king is the head of the hierarchy or suit as the spiritual synthesis and masculine representative, so the queen may be said to be the material synthesis and the chief female representative. So the queen of wands must be, apart from all personality, the representative of banking, exchange, agriculture and of the arts in general, painting, music and dancing in particular.

A cat is seen before the feet of this queen: a remarkable indication of the house in which, as astrology teaches, the moon is exalted. It indicates rightly, that in weak cases there may be some falsehood in the nature of persons indicated by it. Cajolery, but apt to turn into peevishness. Taurus-people are generally good-humored and good-natured, patient, beneficial for their surroundings in material things, but also desirous of luxury and possessions, wealth, riches. In strong cases, there is real virtue.

KNIGHT of WANDS.

Knight of Wands

Divinatory Meanings: Departure, absence, flight, emigration. A dark man. Change of residence. Exploration. The passing of family secrets.

Reversed: Rupture, division, interruption, discord.

He is shown as if upon a journey, armed with a short wand, and although mailed is not on a warlike errand. He is passing mounds or pyramids. The motion of the horse is a key to the character of its rider, and suggests the precipitate mood, or things connected therewith.

In the case of the fourth house the knight relates to family matters or household conditions, eventually the father, to internal conditions in society or groups of people. It must further relate to memories and the past in general, because it means the awakening of the sentiments. The traditional conclusions have been drawn evidently in the negative for the greater part, in consideration of the fact that the sentiments generally are misleading. That they give reason for many changes is quite true. In the case of the twelfth house this is much the same. But extending its result over a much larger circle, the mercurial knight may represent expedition and exploration, discovery, scientific or practical, emigration, estrangement, and the great work of transmigration. It denotes a searching for the unknown, which in weak personal cases may appear as indiscretion or premature revelation, divulgation, profanation.

On account of the twelfth house there is something inimical about him, and a certain dissension of sentiment may find its cause in the past, in a family feud or something in the nature of a misguiding prejudice, tradition, which will have to be given up. A representative of the father, a relative. A man of doubtful though not necessarily bad character. An investigator, occultist, explorer, sailor, wanderer, a guide through strange experiences, vagrant Bohemian type. Disturbing influences and people in general.

Page of Wands

Divinatory Meanings: Dark young man, faithful, a lover, an envoy, a postman. Beside a man, he will bear favorable testimony concerning him. A dangerous rival, if followed by the Page of Cups. Has the chief qualities of his suit. He may signify family intelligence. Young man in search of a lady.

Reversed: Anecdotes, announcements, bad news. Indecision and the instability which accompanies it.

In a scene similar to the former, a young man stands in the act of proclamation. He is unknown but faithful, and his tidings are strange. He is in search of somebody. Possibly a postman or an envoy bringing a message.

The pages always cover the meaning of houses of Air, as we have seen the page of the airy element—wands—is the most airy of them all. The interpretation is easy enough, and the renderings are quite correct, with the exception of one item: we can never see this page as a 'stranger' but rather as an acquaintance, a friend, conforming to the connection with the eleventh house. That with the third house even may bring his personal standing nearer to the querent, for example a brother or schoolmate.

A brother, schoolmate, messenger, postman or envoy, functionary or official of subordinate position, generally a younger man, sometimes on an errand; messages, letters, communications, teaching, instruction, lesson, advertisement, advice, announcement. News.

A friend, some one in business relation with the querent, or with whom he agrees. Telegraph, telephone and wireless. Intuitive connection, telepathy, invention. Helpful influences in general, helpful people of all sorts, tradesmen, purveyors, etc.

Ten of Wands

Divinatory Meanings: Oppression. Fortune, gain, any kind of success, and the oppression of these things. False-seeming and disguise. Loss of a lawsuit. Difficulties and contradictions. Treachery.

Reversed: Contrarieties, difficulties, intrigues, and their analogies.

A man oppressed by the weight of the ten staves which he is carrying. The place which the figure is approaching may suffer from the rods that he carries. Actions and deeds, under the influence of the double-natured mercurial element, may easily degrade into double-dealing and everything else of that nature. But once more it appears to us, that the gypsy tradition is rather too much exclusively on the lower side of things. The qualities mixed here make very often an egoistic blend and a nature which reveals several weaknesses, as soon as it comes under trial.

So the card on the one hand means certainly that the attitude of mind or action will be untrustworthy and must not be relied upon. There is fear and cowardice in it. But on the other hand the combination is that of mental ability, quick perception, etc. It means also the load of the earthy responsibility laid upon the shoulders of an airy creature, consequently *oppression* is a word very much to the point here.

This explains even why weaker natures are driven to undesirable, unreliable actions and reactions by it; they cannot stand the pressure. Strong natures, however, accept the pressure as natural necessity, karma, and carry their burden. This is symbolized by the man carrying the ten wands. It is a symbol of executive ability, production, the doing of necessary things, obedience to official order and rule; officials, red tape and burdens that appear heavier than they actually are.

Nine of Wands

Divinatory Meanings: Obstacle, delay, suspense, adversity, slowness, contrariety, calamity, misfortune, trouble. Revolution, excitement of people. Teaching.

Reversed: Obstacles, adversity, calamity. Generally speaking, a bad card.

The figure leans upon his staff and has an expectant look, as if awaiting an enemy. Behind are eight other staves—erect, in orderly disposition, like a palisade. The card signifies strength in opposition. If attacked, the person will meet an onslaught boldly. With this main significance there are all its possible adjuncts—delay, suspension, adjournment.

This card seems to be queerly veiled. It is at least strange to find only malific expressions of the co-ordination of the element Air and the principle of mind with the house of Sagittarius, the thinker. This looks as if the patrons of the Tarot system did not think it wise to tell much about this sign of the prophets to the fortune-telling gypsies. How this may be does not concern. us any further.

Evidently the card must have to do with prophecy, fortune-telling, teaching, conducting, guiding and the persons of guides, teachers, masters; it must give the notion of traveling and far-reaching schemes, the faculty of speaking foreign languages and of writing, but it is true, that the persons indicated by this card find their strength in opposition and very often therefore are in search of some convenient opponent or opposing force. It means intellectual chasing, sport, hunting, journalism and the raising of spirits, that are not easily to be got rid of afterwards. The latter fact accounts for all that has been said about obstacles, etc.

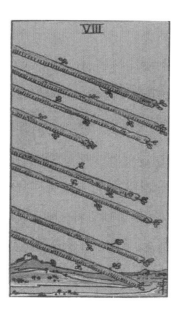

Eight of Wands

Divinatory Meanings: Activity in undertakings, the path of such activity, swiftness, as that of an express messenger. Great haste, great hope, speed towards an end which promises assured felicity. Generally, that which is on the move. The arrows of love or passion. Examination, regrets.

Reversed: Arrows of jealousy, internal dispute, stinging of conscience, quarrels. Domestic disputes for persons who are married.

The card represents motion through the immovable: a flight of wands through an open country; but they draw to the term of their course. That which they signify is at hand; it may be even on the threshold.

The "arrows of love" actually mean passion, and the "arrows of jealousy," the common counterpart of the same. The sensation of sex is born in this house and indicated by this card. As to swift or speedy messages, this may sometimes happen, because the Scorpion is sometimes very sudden in its movements. What the card should have to do with country life is less evident. We should say rather that it must stand in relation with the sea, fishermen and sailors. The mind in this house is very critical and sharp-witted, sometimes subject to doubt and misgivings, superstition and jealousy. It is in search of truth and enjoyment. Artistic abilities will run along the line of poetry, music and sculpture. It has always to do with the hidden side of things, the interior, or the inner life.

Seven of Wands

Divinatory Meanings: Valor, success. Intellectual discussion, wordy strife. Negotiations, war of trade, barter, competition.

Reversed: Perplexity, embarrassments, anxiety. It is also a caution against indecision.

A young man on a craggy eminence brandishing a staff; six other staves are raised towards him from below. It is a card of valor—for six are attacking one, who has the vantage position. It is further a card of success, for the combatant is on the top and his enemies may be unable to reach him.

Six of Wands

Divinatory Meanings: A victor triumphing, great news. Expectation crowned with its own desire. **Reversed:** Apprehension, fear. Treachery, disloyalty. Indefinite delay.

A laureled horseman bears one staff adorned with a laurel crown; footmen with staves are at his side. The element of thought on the earthy house of Virgo must naturally bring forth knowledge of every detail and reveal mistakes or shortcomings; it promotes efficiency, and the latter is one of the principal meanings of the card. Here again is a double mercurial expression, so this card must denote special abilities, capacities, technical insight; moreover food questions and medicine, medicaments and nursing; practical arrangement of details, but as Virgo "kills the prophets," this card may contain some or other discrepancy in the philosophical or logical, theoretical or strictly just side of things.

Five of Wands

Divinatory Meanings: Imitation. The struggle for riches and gain, gold. Self-centeredness.

Reversed: Litigation, disputes, trickery, contradiction. Quarrels turned to advantage.

A posse of youths, who are brandishing staves, as if in sport or strife. It is mimic warfare, but also the strenuous competition and struggle of the search after riches and fortune. In this sense it connects with the battle of life.

Speaking and thinking to such a self-centered way, that no notice is taken of other people's standpoint; consequently clashing of opinions; sometimes it may allude to gold and presents, but to the promise rather than to the fact. There is little or no evil in this card. At most it may denote stupid and childish persistence in one's own personal opinion. It has something sunny in it and is good for health and wealth in a general way, promoting both, but it is not riches in itself.

Four of Wands

Divinatory Meanings: Country life, haven of refuge, domestic harvest, family, concord, harmony, prosperity, peace, and the perfected work of these. Unexpected good fortune. Theatrical arts.

Reversed: Prosperity, increase, felicity, beauty, embellishment. Beautiful children.

From the four great staves planted in the foreground there is a great garland suspended; two female figures uplift nosegays; at their side is a bridge over a moat, leading to an old manorial house.

The expression of the common motive, of that which binds people together. It is not the contract, but the motive which afterwards leads to contracts, or from which the contract will result. A common mistake, in astrological descriptions as well, is this mixing up of definitions relating to the cause and to the effect respectively. Mercury brooding over the house of the family and the moon, engenders homely feelings, memories, thoughts of internal service, household matters, and tends more or less to a profane and familiar or descriptive language, to joke, fun and the theatrical art, to inviting people to come together and have their share in weal and woe.

Three of Wands

Divinatory Meanings: Strength, enterprise, effort, commerce, discovery. A very good card. Collaboration in business will be beneficial.

Reversed: The end of troubles, suspension or cessation of adversity, toil and disappointment.

A calm, stately personage, with his back turned, looking from a cliff's edge at ships passing over the sea. Three staves are planted in the ground, and he leans slightly on one of them. Those are his ships, bearing his merchandise, which are sailing over the sea. The card also signifies able co-operation in business, as if the successful merchant prince were looking from his side towards yours with a view to help you.

Two of Wands

Divinatory Meanings: No marriage possible. Riches, fortune, magnificence. Physical suffering, disease, chagrin, sadness.

Reversed: Surprise, wonder, enchantment, emotion, trouble, fear.

A tall man looks from a battlemented roof over sea and shore; he holds a globe in his right hand, while a staff in his left rests on the battlement; another is fixed in a ring. Here is a lord overlooking his dominion and alternately contemplating a globe; it looks like the malady, the mortification, the sadness of Alexander amidst the grandeur of this world's wealth. It is the impression of heaviness, of a load on the back, which easily may attain the more concise form of a fear, a gloom, a feeling of being downcast, impotent, weak and not able to resist circumstances. So it may signify the pressure of material conditions, the responsibility imparted by riches, but also projects or conceptions of an economical nature and the idea of capital and capitalizing.

Further the combination of the principles of air with the house of Taurus must give music, and we may be sure that this card always has some significance in that way and in the sphere of art intellectually and in general. This is a very important significance.

Ace of Wands

Divinatory Meanings: Creation, invention, enterprise, principle, beginning, source. Birth, family, origin. The starting point of enterprises. Money, fortune, inheritance.

Reversed: Fall, decadence, ruin, perdition, to perish also a certain clouded joy. A sign of birth.

A hand issuing from a cloud grasps a stout wand or club with leaves falling from the wand to the Earth. The cards of the airy element have always and in every instance a double meaning and not only in the sense of right and reversed, but a meaning on two sides. And apparently this has been wrongly introduced as right or reversed in some cases. So the ace of wands will represent the effect of suddenness, of the incidental, even accidental. It denotes something that is making its appearance all of a sudden; a sort of manifestation, creation such as the birth of a child. This, by the way, is generally considered to be a joy for the parents, but may not be for the soul, which has to accept once more the limitations of life in a body of earth.

King of Cups

Divinatory Meanings: Fair man, man of business, law, or divinity. Responsible, disposed to oblige the Querent. Equity, art and science, those who profess science, law and art. Creative intelligence.

Reversed: Dishonest, double-dealing man. Roguery, injustice, vice, scandal, pillage, considerable loss.

He holds a short scepter in his left hand and a great cup in his right; his throne is set upon the sea; on one side a ship is riding and on the other a dolphin is leaping. The implicit is that the Sign of the Cup naturally refers to water, which appears in all the court cards.

This king is the chief of the kingdom of the soul, coming on the Ninth house, and consequently must indicate the teacher, prophet, man of law and divinity; the professor, inspirer and great traveller; sometimes a hunter, a wanderer, or a sailor, a yachtsman. Honesty and probity will be generally his characteristics, but some fantasy may be mixed with it and he may be less particular in details or accuracy. He may be exuberant or even excessive, and this may cause some excitement, but we see nothing of scandal, vice, thievishness or anything of that kind in this card.

There is a lively sentiment of justice in it and the person indicated by it will certainly be disposed to render justice to the querent, whether he be connected with the law or not. If the querent is himself a weak or vicious individual, the card may indicate the judge before whom he has to appear. At all events it may represent the idea of judgment of the querent's actions or business. Further there is less of science in this card than of philosophy, which is quite another department. There is the idea of promoting, inspiring, pushing. There lies promise for the future and likeliness of monetary advance in this Sagittarian card.

QUEEN of CUPS.

Queen of Cups

Divinatory Meanings: Good, fair woman. Honest, devoted woman, who will do service to the Querent. Loving intelligence, and hence the gift of vision. Success, happiness, pleasure. Wisdom, virtue. A perfect spouse and a good mother.

Reversed: A good woman; otherwise, distinguished woman but one not to be trusted; perverse woman; vice, dishonor, depravity. A rich marriage.

Beautiful, fair, dreamy—as one who sees visions in a cup. This is, however, only one of her aspects; she sees, but she also acts, and her activity feeds her dream. This queen is to us the image of the married woman and the mother and of all that which woman can give to man and mankind, by her virtue both of soul and body. So the card must also mean the realization of hopes and wishes, consequently success. The wisdom is here more of the practical blend, usefulness, knowing how to act with care and prudence.

The card may represent a woman, or an impersonal power or authority, whom the querent has to obey, or to whom it will be to his advantage to submit. It expresses a tendency to go out into the world and make a name and position for oneself, and indicates the right moment to do so. It is fairly certain that it will ensure some publicity, renown, fame, or even glory or theatrical success, but of 'scandal' we see no indication whatever in the card itself, though of course publicity connected with very evil influences might end in something like that. In such cases, however, we must not ascribe the effect to the card, which means publicity, but to that of the evil influences.

Knight of Cups

Divinatory Meanings: Arrival, approach of a friend or messenger. Advances, proposition, invitation, incitement.

Reversed: Trickery, artifice, subtlety, swindling, duplicity, fraud.

Graceful, but not warlike; riding quietly, wearing a winged helmet, referring to those higher graces of the imagination which sometimes characterize this card. He too is a dreamer, but the images of the side of sense haunt him in his vision.

Though the cups never go to anything like hatred or crime or real malice, their weakness is in being unreliable or incalculable with regard to things of the exact world or matter. So in the worst cases this card may indicate everything connected with swindling from sheer mental instability. But it may also be, that the term swindler is wrongly given to people who are standing apart from the common herd and are more or less occultists.

There may be certainly a considerable degree of falsehood expressed by this card: false interpretation, misjudgment, tendencious or fantastic narratives, exaggerated complaints, imaginary wrongs, pathos and what the world calls miscarriage. On account of the eighth house all this may be connected with sex-questions or intimate and private affairs. The card may express indiscretion committed and slanderous reports, secretly promulgated. It has to do with secrets and the divulgation of secrets. But there may be also a higher sway in the emotional realm: devotion, sacrifice, charity.

There is much occultism in this card; this Knight may be unknown or anonymous but a very important messenger (to the soul?) At its best he is Saint George killing the dragon, the Rosicrucian brother.

PAGE of CUPS.

Page of Cups

Divinatory Meanings: Fair young man, one impelled to render service and with whom the Querent will be connected. A studious youth. News, message. Application, reflection, meditation.

Reversed: Taste, inclination, attachment, seduction, deception, artifice.

A fair, pleasing, somewhat effeminate page, of studious and intent aspect, contemplates a fish rising from a cup to look at him. It is the pictures of the mind taking form.

The Page or servant, messenger, of the cups suit has to do with friendship and relations, e.g. marriage. He must be the friend who brings inviting messages, seductive proposals, if not of formal marriage, perhaps of some love-affair or jolly gathering, sportive meeting, or intellectual entertainment, lecture, etc. It is not quite impossible, that the idea of seduction is connected with it or at least a strong sense of persuasion.

If it relates to news, there is emotion in it, news that will affect the feelings in some way or other. Relations will be of a passing nature, but may be very pleasant. The combination of the Water with the Air generally adds much to the instruction, development or education of people So there must be much of all this in the Page of Cups. The effects do not always bear the characteristic of reliability, nor of permanence.

Ten of Cups

Divinatory Meanings: Contentment, repose of the entire heart. Perfection of human love and friendship. The town, village or country inhabited by the Querent.

Reversed: A serious argument, indignation, violence.

Appearance of Cups in a rainbow; it is contemplated in wonder and ecstasy by a man and woman below, evidently husband and wife. His right arm is about her, his left is raised upward, she raises her right arm. The two children dancing near them have not observed the prodigy but are happy after their own manner. There is a home-scene beyond.

Now what about the town or city? Virgo is "the city which killed the prophets" (Jerusalem) and the addiction originally will have indicated the physical, sensual embodiment of the soul, in which the spirit is buried or killed as the mystic formula has it. This card may therefore be called, with truth, the indication of 'the city of God' which, by analogy, becomes the physical body, as well as one's residence or native land. It means the physical possession or ownership.

Consequently it has to do with the agreeable sensation of being at home and at ease, having possession of what is wanted. It must also mean being fully acquainted with one's work. Good health and wise living.

Nine of Cups

Divinatory Meanings: Concord, contentment. Victory, success, advantage. Satisfaction for the Querent or person for whom the consultation is made. Success for military men.

Reversed: Truth, loyalty, liberty. Mistakes, imperfections.

A goodly personage has feasted to his heart's content, and abundant refreshment of wine is on the arched counter behind him, seeming to indicate that the future is also assured. The picture offers the material side only, but there are other aspects.

The card must signify the realization of hopes and wishes lying in one's own power or destiny, making one enjoy the fulness of life, and adopting the philosophy of Epicurus. There is no evil in it. It shows goodness and a jovial disposition, not only contentment and happiness in one's self, but also, owing to Leo's influence, the love of bestowing hospitality on other people and helping them.

Eight of Cups

Divinatory Meanings: Giving joy, mildness, timidity, honor, modesty. The decline of a matter, or that a matter which has been thought to be important is really of slight consequence—either for good or evil. End of a business enterprise. Change in home life.

Reversed: Great joy, happiness, feasting. Perfect satisfaction.

A man of dejected aspect is deserting the cups of his family or intimate circle, enterprise, undertaking or previous concern. Changes in home-life, be it for the better or for the worse. There cannot be much of order or rule in this combination, and disorder or chaos is threatened. The strong Cancerian peculiarities, such as shyness, timidity, prudishness, may appear here.

Feelings, sentiments, wishes have very little chance of becoming reality in this house, and this may be called the true reason for leaving the house. The latter seems to us to be the proper meaning: either leaving the safe and comfortable home, or losing the chance to realize more ambitious projects. Being the eighth card of the suit, it may denote a girl, and cups are said to be related to the fair or blonde type.

Seven of Cups

Divinatory Meanings: Fairy favors, images of reflection, sentiment, imagination, things seen in the glass of contemplation; some attainment in these degrees, but nothing permanent or substantial.

Reversed: Desire, will, determination, project.

Strange chalices of vision, but the images are more especially those of the fantastic spirit. The changeful concrete mind and thought in which indeed nothing is permanent, and everything is passing. These effects must be varied, including the most fantastic plans and conceptions, and *fancy* is the most fitting word for this card. It will denote many intellectual proceedings and has to do with traveling for short distances, sight-seeing, considering, gathering impressions. The card represents the conditions of mind in which the surroundings are simply reflected in the soul. There may come seductive and suggestive images, some of which may be realized, but others will remain just fancy. The fairy favors may serve to mislead man.

Much in this card will not come to physical fruition.

Six of Cups

Divinatory Meanings: A card of the past and of memories, looking back
childhood. Happiness, enjoyment, but coming from the past. Things that have vanishe
Another reading reverses this, giving new relations, new knowledge, new environme
and then the children are disporting in an unfamiliar precinct.

Reversed: The future, renewal, that which will come to pass presently.

Children in an old garden, their cups filled with flowers. It relates to t
country, and in connection with the latter the card will indicate rustic pleasur
enjoyment of country life and restoration to health by residence on the land. Happiness
surely a characteristic of this card, but we should say particularly in a simple and count
life. Further we ascribe much artistic value to it, especially in painting, love for t
picturesque. It means receptivity for beautiful impressions in general. On the other ha
it may denote a love of good cheer and feasting. Good health and good humor a
certainly results of this combination.

On account of the Taurian qualities it will impart the tendency to collect objec
of art and of antiquarian value; also an instinctive understanding of the same, so
promotes dealing in such objects. Appreciation of music in the lighter style, love of th
theatre, but love of Nature above all.

Five of Cups

Divinatory Meanings: It is a card of loss, but something remains over. It is a card of inheritance, patrimony, transmission, but not corresponding to expectations. A card of marriage, but not without bitterness or frustration.

Reversed: News, alliances, affinity, consanguinity, ancestry, return, false projects.

A dark, cloaked figure, looking sideways at three prone cups two others stand upright behind him. There has been a loss: three have been taken, but two are left; a bridge is in the background, leading to a small keep or holding. Family matters will come naturally to the querent in this case, just as they were swept from him or evaded by him in the preceding one. Still we cannot see, that the card should denote the members of the family in particular.

Now family-matters may include inheritance as well as marriage, but so many other things may also be included that it is difficult to enumerate them, and none of them is indicated particularly. So we do not think it wise to say anything more definitely about this. The water of the feelings coming on the ascendant indicates sensitiveness and emotion, which may bring sorrow or pleasure, but generally mixed experiences and not without care. There may be material losses in consequence.

Four of Cups

Divinatory Meanings: Weariness, disgust, aversion, imaginary vexations, as if the wine of this world had caused satiety only; another wine, as if a fairy gift, is now offered the wastrel, but he sees no consolation therein. This is also a card of blended pleasure.

Reversed: Novelty, presage, new instruction, new relations.

A young man is seated under a tree and contemplates three cups set on the grass before him; an arm issuing from a cloud offers him another cup. His expression is one of discontent with his environment, certainly, but at the same time it shows the querent throwing his future on the waters of new adventure—leaving home and family to wander forth towards new experiences, enlarging the horizon of his views. There may be some ailment of the soul, however, in this house and in very weak cases alienation even. Sentiments not reciprocated, nor understood. A feeling of being outside one's proper environment.

There may be encounters with strangers or foreigners, and discoveries, as results of discontent or dissatisfaction with present conditions. So in relation to these conditions it may mean: failing to understand or to appreciate things as they are, estrangement of the world, which may lead to seclusion or secluded feelings.

Three of Cups

Divinatory Meanings: The conclusion of any matter in plenty, perfection and merriment; happy issue, victory, fulfillment, solace, healing. Unexpected advancement.

Reversed: Expedition, dispatch, achievement. End of business. It signifies also the side of excess in physical enjoyment, and the pleasures of the senses.

Maidens in a garden-ground with cups uplifted, as if pledging one another in friendship or success. There is no feeling whatever of being hampered or thwarted, or depressed. All goes well and the general sensation is cheerful. It is the sign of a good time, good luck and general satisfaction. As the eleventh house also rules the blood, it is very favorable for health and eventual recuperation. Moreover this house has to do with commerce and business, and the card favors them beyond a doubt, giving a good understanding of opportunity and of the character and wishes of those with whom we have to do, so that we can supply what they ask.

Two of Cups

Divinatory Meanings: Love, passion, friendship, affinity, union, concord, sympathy, the interrelation of the sexes.

Reversed: Passion, lust, desire.

A youth and maiden are pledging one another, and above their cups rises the Caduceus of Hermes, between the great wings of which there appears a lion's head. It is a variant of a sign which is found in a few old examples of this card. Some curious emblematical meanings are attached to it, but they do not concern us in this place.

The two souls find each other here in an act, which of course must be that of meeting in the body. Soul-union, ending in bodily attraction. So the traditional rendering appears once more to be fairly correct. It is the outcome of idealism, indicated by the ace, shared by two souls. It is anyhow not the sex-element as a curse, but as a blessing in practical life. The card may further denote any sort of friendly act and sympathetic encounter. We should say, as regards love, it is to be rather defined as love-making, courting.

Ace of Cups

Divinatory Meanings: House of the true heart, joy, content, abode, nourishment, abundance, fertility. Holy Table. Inflexible will or law.
Reversed: House of the false heart, mutation, instability, revolution.

The waters are beneath, and thereon are water-lilies. The hand issues from the cloud, holding in its palm the cup, from which four streams are pouring. A dove, bearing in its bill a cross-marked Host, descends to place the Wafer in the Cup while the dew of water is falling on all sides. It is an intimation of that which may lie behind the Lesser Arcana.

KING of SWORDS.

King of Swords

Divinatory Meanings: Judgment, law, and all its connexions. Power, command, authority, militant intelligence, offices of the crown. A lawyer, senator, or doctor.
Reversed: Cruelty, perversity, barbarity, perfidy, evil intention.

The King of Swords sits in judgment, holding the unsheathed sign of his suit. He recalls, of course, the conventional Symbol of justice in the Trumps Major, and he may represent this virtue, but he is rather the power of life and death, in virtue of his office.

Whatsoever we may say of the *reversed* side or weaker cases of this card, a king is a king and always denotes a higher accord, some one or something of principal value and rank. The king of the Martian element naturally is the king of matter and of war—also he who wins war and conducts the battle of earthy interests. It denotes the dominion and rulership of this element, consequently the military chief.

As the ruler of the ascendant, the card may certainly mean any person heading a cycle of material activity and before all a pioneer on this plane, an independent man living on his own means. While material integrity is implicit, duplicity, doubt, double-dealing or uncertainty are definitely excluded. It indicates material certainty and severity, whether beneficial or malific from a personal point of view, healthy or rude, even cruel. But we fail to see what it has to do with perversity, unless the meaning be the overruling of everything else, the higher by the material power, and the misuse of the latter.

The card means an emphatic YES.

Queen of Swords

Divinatory Meanings: Widowhood, female sadness and embarrassment, absence, sterility, mourning, privation, separation. Art in general.

Reversed: Malice, bigotry, artifice, prudery, bale, deceit. A woman with ill-will.

The Queen's right hand raises the weapon vertically and the hilt rests on an arm of her royal chair the left hand is extended, the arm raised her countenance is severe but chastened; it suggests familiarity with sorrow. It does not represent mercy, and, her sword notwithstanding, she is scarcely a symbol of power.

This card must mean either woman ruling by matter, material or magnetic attraction, purely physical charm, or ruled by material elements herself. The latter may be seen as: ruled by the desire of luxury and money, or as: overpowered by material difficulties, weighed down under the burden of a material world. A woman of Saturnian and Martian qualities is seldom charming unless in a purely physical and sexual way; there may be higher virtues, however, which in this case will be developed by suffering, such as chastity, severity, continence—from which it will be easily seen, that sterility, privation and mourning may derive, personally.

On the one hand this card may be a woman under affliction and severed from her natural protector or protection—widow, divorced, separated, though not the unmarried; on the other hand we have to see in this card the woman who is paid for her love, and the fact that "woman costs money," a fact of more occult significance than the world at large understands.

Well aspected, it may indicate art in general and sometimes wealth after assiduous struggle and toil.

KNIGHT of SWORDS.

Knight of Swords

Divinatory Meanings: Skill, bravery, capacity. Wrath, war, destruction, opposition, resistance, ruin. A soldier, man of arms. Heroic action in the future.

Reversed: Imprudence, incapacity, extravagance. Struggle that will be conquered.

The Knight is riding in full course, as if scattering his enemies. In the design he is really a prototypical hero of romantic chivalry. He might almost be Galahad, whose sword is swift and sure because he is clean of heart. The armed man under the rule of the Emperor, the military man who may rather fall under the same house as the police, and be indicated by the page of swords.

Another significance of this card is that of painful memories, suffering by ancient wrongs. In fact war is in all cases, be it private or collective, the phenomenon of the outbreak of some ancient wrong or evil—the wrong of oppression on one side or the evil of desire on the other. The Knight of swords must bear the significance of the bearer of weapons, which avenge wrongs or serve attacks. Badly aspected it may mean opposition against the power of the father or the Emperor, revolution, which is quite in the line of the grumbling and malcontent nature of the Cancerian of the lower type. It is however, to be expected that such opposition will be very much hidden, dark, in the background, not open nor very loyal.

On account of its relation with the twelfth house this card may also mean a surgeon and operations performed by him, and, in lower types or weaker cases, fraud and destruction of organisms, whatever these may be. It may further relate here to all sorts of bad passions and to degrees of hatred.

Page of Swords

Divinatory Meanings: Authority, overseeing, secret service, vigilance, spying, examination, and the qualities thereto belonging. An artist, learned man, or a spy.

Reversed: More evil side of these qualities; what is unforeseen, unprepared state; sickness is also intimated. Astonishing news. Improvisation.

A lithe, active figure holds a sword upright in both hands, while in the act of swift walking. He is passing over rugged land, and about his way the clouds are collocated wildly. He is alert and lithe, looking this way and that, as if an expected enemy might appear at any moment.

It is justly indicated by tradition, that the Martian and Saturnian Gemini-man is a specialist in unlawful knowledge or in knowledge gathered at the cost of much trouble and effort; so it may be also knowledge gathered later in life, university extension. Exact intellectual results may appear as: remarks, observations, or notes. When put in the negative there may be investigation, examination, etc. All these are truly the effects of Gemini.

On account of the eleventh house we shall have to note the same sort of results but more or less reciprocal and sudden, whereas Uranus, lord of this house, accelerates the energy of Mars in this element but is apt to destroy the Saturnian vibrations or at least counteract them. It is quite true, therefore, that this card may represent speaking and acting without sufficient preparation and without dogmatic or very formal outlines: improvisation.

This page, on account of its eleventh house relations, will represent the railway, tramway, or bus-conductor as well as the constable regulating the traffic, also the warnings of the same.

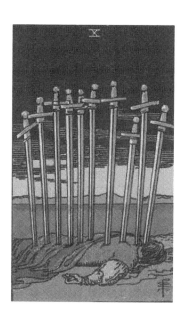

Ten of Swords

Divinatory Meanings: Whatsoever is intimated by the design; also pain, affliction, tears, sadness, desolation. Imprisonment. Treason. *It is not a card indicating violent death.*

Reversed: Advantage, profit, success, victory, but none of these are permanent; also power and authority.

A prostrate figure, pierced by all the swords belonging to the card. The card represents material necessity and the limits and corner-stones which it erects. It is ultimately the card of inescapable karmic results, or material karma itself. To the profane this very often means affliction, and the personality may be burdened by the weight of fate. The image of this card seems to suggest this burden.

On the other hand tradition is certainly not wrong in stating that it may represent gain and profit, as the card of karma will bring the full measure of material things in general and not only in the way of tragedy. Profit and advantage, however, may also become oppressive and its possibility must be considered here.

Nine of Swords

Divinatory Meanings: Death, failure, delay, deception, disappointment, despair. A priest. A bad omen. Intolerance.

Reversed: Imprisonment, suspicion, doubt, reasonable fear, shame.

A woman sitting upright on her bed holding her head in her hands in a state of lamentation, with the swords over her. She knows no sorrow like hers. It is a card of utter desolation.

From the essence of this card arises inquisition and every sort of intolerance, religious intolerance above all, because the materialistic mind thinks itself in possession of the only expression of Truth, and condemns every other. So this card may also indicate all sorts of hard judgment, rigid attitudes of mind, orthodoxy. For this indeed is the meaning of materialism in religion and ethics. When the material expression of truth and ideals is at its height, it reaches the value of rite and ritual or religious ceremony, which at its best stands in relation to dogmatism as the jewel to simple stones or dry sand.

Eight of Swords

Divinatory Meanings: Bad news, crisis, censure, conflict, calumny, sickness.

Reversed: Disquiet, difficulty, opposition, accident, treachery. Departure of a relative.

A woman, bound and hoodwinked, with the swords of the card about her. Yet it is a card of temporary hardship rather than of irretrievable bondage. The image drawn on this card may well indicate the blindness of man amidst the dangers of this world and of his own desire-nature. It must indicate physical sex-nature above all. Further, we shall find everything relating to the revenge of matter upon spirit, the latter being bound and blinded by the former, consequently everything in the nature of obstacles and hindrances, pain and affliction.

The house of avenging justice may well cause a condemnation, or a sickness which is the result of sinning against nature's laws; patience is required where this card rules and endurance will save the position. In its most general sense it means the binding by the laws of matter, suffering from the lack of money, impotence by debt or material want, poverty. It may be a great strain on the feelings. As the eight of each suit is accepted as indicating some feminine influence to which we are ready to subscribe, there will be danger from an acquisitive girl or uncouth female here, or even sickness through same. As far as material laws are compelling in this world, there must be fatality in this card, or at least something from which there will be no physical escape.

Seven of Swords

Divinatory Meanings: Design, attempt, wish, hope, confidence. Quarreling, a plan that may fail, annoyance.

Reversed: Good advice neglected, counsel, instruction, slander, babbling.

A man in the act of carrying away five swords rapidly; the two others of the card remain stuck in the ground. A camp is close at hand.

Owing to the diplomatic and fox-like qualities of the house of Libra, the querent may, by this card, attempt to steal the weapons of the opponent, as the figure suggests: using the arguments and fighting with the weapons of the enemy. The card must indicate everything in the line of material ability, from the science of the use of tools, crafts and arts up to tricks of abuse. It may equally favor a laborer, an engineer, a dentist, a surgeon and a burglar.

Six of Swords

Divinatory Meanings: Journey by water. Route, road. Pleasant voyage. An envoy.

Reversed: Declaration, confession, publicity. Proposal of love. Unfavorable lawsuit.

A ferryman carrying passengers in his punt to the further shore. The course is smooth, and seeing that the freight is light, it may be noted that the work is not beyond his strength.

It must be the way or path leading out into the world from our house or living place. This explains what tradition says about envoy and emigration, though the latter is somewhat far-fetched. But it is true that the effect of that which this card represents may go far and in general signifies the message in the sphere of matter (Mercury is lord of this house), the message materialized. The message is conveyed by means of the way or the path.

It may also, however, be the passing over to that side, the crossing of the Styx, which seems to be indicated by the picture of this card. The cusp of the seventh house in the horoscope is the end, in the same way as the ascendant is the beginning. Though tradition has not rendered it so, this card must in many instances have the significance of passing away.

Five of Swords

Divinatory Meanings: Destruction, infamy, dishonor, loss. Bitterness toward the world.

Reversed: The same. Burial and mourning.

A disdainful man looks after two retreating and dejected figures. Their swords lie upon the ground. He carries two others on his left shoulder, and a third sword is in his right hand, point to earth. He is the master in possession of the field.

The element of Earth with its influence of Mars and Saturn on the Fifth house, ruling the heart, is certain to lead to a feeling of being wronged by the world, an inner bitterness and impotence, which hinders enterprise and business; so these will suffer. The heart itself, being of precisely the opposite nature, will suffer and find things awkward, horrible, and hideous. However, he may be the master of the field if his inner force is great enough to conquer the afflictions which assail him. In other words, it need not be a card of absolute defeat, for there may very well be a good result, but nevertheless it denotes serious difficulty and a critical moment or period in life, in which the querent or some one to whom it relates will be threatened with the above-mentioned sad effects.

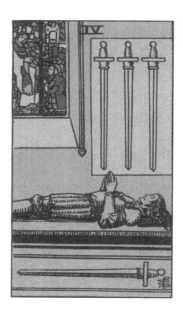

Four of Swords

Divinatory Meanings: Vigilance, retreat, solitude, hermit's repose, exile. Tomb and coffin.

Reversed: Wise administration, circumspection, economy, avarice, precaution, testament.

The effigy of a knight in the attitude of prayer, at full length upon his tomb. This card has been said to stand for economy, savings, even avarice and household affairs as well as for many things in connection with the end of life, since the fourth house in the horoscope relates to the end of life, and to the inner side of life as long as this lasts.

If this card should relate to business, it certainly does not mean that anything like accord has been or will be reached, but that one of the parties retires or takes his proposals back. It may also relate to the condition of the soul, in which one harvests the results of material life in the world, whether spiritually, by meditation, or materially, by economy.

In any case it points to a stillness and heavy condition of the mind. Further, to the tendency of collecting, gathering.

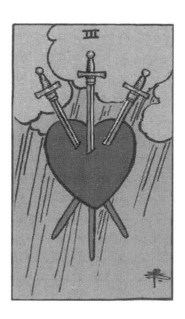

Three of Swords

Divinatory Meanings: Removal, absence, delay. Oppression, worry. Bad news. Affliction.

Reversed: Mental alienation, error, loss, distraction, disorder, confusion.

Three swords piercing a heart with a cloud and rain behind. The element of Earth on the Third house acts in the way of the mind and mental processes, and must appear as troubles because it gives the feeling of the mind being burdened, which might easily go as far as oppression. If the burden becomes too heavy, either the body or the soul may suffer severely, and pain, affliction or mental aberration may ensue.

This card must generally mean bad news too, the message which brings news of the affliction. It may be a corrective to a too easy and volatile imagination. It will in most cases denote some sickness, as a result of the pressure or oppressed feeling in the mind or a circumstances in general. It may be the result of worrying. The house of Gemini also suggests some suffering on account of distance, separateness, being far from one other.

The oppressed mind, which cannot have its way, may easily denote the spiritual condition of a nun or some one who takes refuge within the precincts of a monastery. In this case, however, the motives are not of the more elevated or exalted order: there is spitefulness, vexation, bitterness on account of unrealized hopes, want of idealism. So this does not indicate the idealistic type of monasticism. The card typifies the worries of the lesser sort of mind, also small talk, evil thought, the wrestling of the inferior mind with matter and all that may be expected from it.

Two of Swords

Divinatory Meanings: Friendship, courage. Tenderness, affection. Artistic appreciation.

Reversed: Imposture, falsehood, duplicity, disloyalty.

A hoodwinked female figure balances two swords upon her shoulders. It denotes artistic appreciation, founded on the perfect functioning of the senses. Taste for art will be born from this and an exact knowledge of prices and values. It is the card which means quality and essential virtue. Therefore it has been rendered as falsehood when reversed—when the innate virtue is wanting.

In weak cases this card will certainly denote sensuality and lazy luxurious habits, which will be found accompanied in many instances by the desire for money. For the rest we see in such cases the possibility of stupid resistance, dullness, cruelty, relentless opposition and recreation, passive obstruction, perhaps silent, unforgiving hatred. In another respect it means the will to cultivate the soil, in the literal as well as in the figurative sense.

Ace of Swords

Divinatory Meanings: Triumph, the excessive degree in everything, conquest, triumph of force. It is a card of great force, in love as well as in hatred. Great prosperity or great misery.

Reversed: The same, but the results are disastrous. Conception, childbirth. Broken marriage.

A hand issues from a cloud, grasping as word, the point of which is encircled by a crown. This has to do with a beginning, a strong outpouring of force, an impulse, and a material one too. Positive activity on the material plane is typically masculine, and this is a very masculine card, perhaps the most of all. There is no negotiation possible with it. It is emphatically *yes* o r *no*. One of the primary expressions of the masculine is fructification, and the male action is indicated by this card. For the same reason it means seed and its natural consequence is conception and childbirth, the ace indicating here also the ascendant.

In everything this card means the actual beginning in material execution, which at the same time may cut short something else. It signifies of course a decision, the end of uncertainty or twilight. It is a fresh starting point in matter: *alea jacta est* (the die is cast). It may as well mean a strong demand, an appeal. There is courage in it and firm initiative. It may cause pain and affliction, but annihilates doubt, the greatest torture.

King of Pentacles

Divinatory Meanings: Valor. Business and normal intellectual aptitude, sometimes mathematical gifts and attainments of this kind. Success. A rather dark man, a merchant, master, professor. Agreement and consent.

Reversed: Vice, weakness, ugliness, perversity, corruption, peril.

The figure calls for no special description the face is rather dark, suggesting also courage, but somewhat lethargic in tendency. The bull's head should be noted as a recurrent symbol on the throne. The sign of this suit is represented throughout as engraved or blazoned with the pentagram, typifying the correspondence of the four elements in human nature and that by which they may be governed. In many old Tarot packs this suit stood for coins or money, but the consensus of divinatory meanings is on the side of some change, because the cards do not happen to deal especially with questions of money.

The King is the higher octave of the ace, and this particular king heads the cross of fixed signs, so has to do with economy, agriculture, art, vast business, devotional service of the church. The general effect of this card must consequently be to afford protection, and as it shows a very favorable attitude on the part of superiors or influential people, though these will be rather young, or at least, not very old. There is above all noblesse in this card, integrity, honesty above all doubt, nor is anything in it which can be turned to evil, were it thrice reversed.

The only sort of faults that could be observed in people coming under it would be pride coupled with some vanity, love of pomp, gambling. The Leo-type will naturally dominate the card. Here is a man whom you must go to see and visit, because he will never come to you. He has a widespread influence, which is for the good of everybody who wishes to profit by it, and against which it is hopeless to contend.

QUEEN of PENTACLES

Queen of Pentacles

Divinatory Meanings: Opulence, generosity, magnificence, security, liberty. Happy marriage. Presents from a rich relative. A dark woman who is helpful.

Reversed: Evil, suspicion, suspense, fear, mistrust.

The face suggests that of a dark woman, whose qualities might be summed up in the idea of greatness of soul; she has also the serious cast of intelligence; she contemplates her symbol and may see worlds therein.

This must be a woman always inclined to help and to serve, to make herself useful, a nurse perhaps, a household woman of good standing a good hostess. There are also qualities of science in this house, as it is the house of the Academy and Minerva. So she may be as an incarnation of Minerva herself, protecting science and craftsmanship as the Queen of Wands protects the arts. She must have many qualities and above all refinement, though she may suffer more or less from the evil—so far as it can be called—of doubt, and the difficulty of choosing between many possibilities in her nature. She is generous and beneficial. Her presence is a good augury and she brings always protection and material wealth or at least well-being, ruling this house of earth.

There may be some timidity; there is always honesty, honorable action, correctness and the right attitude to all problems of life, discretion, education, understanding, knowledge. These qualities certainly engender security in life.

Knight of Pentacles

Divinatory Meanings: Utility, serviceableness, interest, responsibility. A useful man. Useful discoveries. Pleasant memories.

Reversed: Inertia, idleness. Discouragement, carelessness. A brave man unemployed.

The Knight rides a slow, enduring, heavy horse, to which his own aspect corresponds. He exhibits his symbol, but does not look therein. The querent may profit by legacies or inheritance. Consequently the beneficial influence on the weak point in our material conditions may be interpreted as advantage.

The knight is always a personification, too, and we must see him as a person who is obliging, carrying out a will, coming to the aid of the querent, secretly or confidentially perhaps, at least not publicly, visiting him in his house, saving him from material and financial troubles. It may be a loan, inheritance or advance, but without any hard conditions connected with it, so it may be a present. On the other hand, it means the tendency to enjoy the good things of the heart within one's own private or family circle in repose, in some retreat, secretly.

In weak cases there may be some danger of degeneration into idleness or indolence, etc. In connection with the fourth house, ruling family matters and the past, the home and the storehouse.

The card has to do with pleasant memories, recollections, people we have known before; collections and collecting.

Page of Pentacles

Divinatory Meanings: Application, study, scholarship, reflection. News, messages and the bringer thereof. Rule, management. A dark youth. A young officer or soldier. A child.

Reversed: Prodigality, dissipation, liberality, luxury. Unfavorable news.

A youthful figure, looking intently at the pentacle which hovers over his raised hands. He moves slowly, insensible of that which is about him. The Page, always more or less of a messenger, in this case of fiery nature. The card will indicate a proposal of marriage, courting, love-making, but in a gentle, sometimes a poetical or platonic way, not without ardor however.

It has also to do with all sorts of honorable offices and denominations and may indicate any official person in the civil service and commerce, a stationer, bookseller or editor, bookkeeper or director, appointed by the owner or patron.

Ten of Pentacles

Divinatory Meanings: Gain, riches. Family matters, a home, the abode of a family. Artistic value.

Reversed: Chance, fatality, loss, robbery, games of hazard. Sometimes gift, dowry, pension.

A man and woman beneath an archway which gives entrance to a house and domain. They are accompanied by a child, who looks curiously at two dogs accosting an ancient personage seated in the foreground. The child's hand is on one of them.

Naturally this card has to do with economy, gain, and riches; while Taurus, as the vast field of action in the universe, actually procures that which is called opportunity. The influence of Venus and the Sun on the second house is very favorable for art as well as for monetary matters. So this must be a card of a great artistic value, foretelling success in music and painting and an immense love of the beautiful. It indicates possession without drawback or danger. These very intricate constructions themselves however, cannot be under the rule of the vast and monotonously extensive house of Taurus. The card stands for banking or insurance house, and favor both trades: banking and insurance. It promises prosperity by means of economy, agriculture, perhaps art dealing. Further every collective possession.

Nine of Pentacles

Divinatory Meanings: Prudence, safety, success, accomplishment, certitude, discernment.

Reversed: Roguery, deception, voided project. Vain hopes.

A woman, with a bird upon her wrist, stands amidst a great abundance of grapevines in the garden of a manorial house. It is a wide domain, suggesting plenty in all things. Possibly it is her own possession and testifies to material well-being.

This card has a very positive in its meaning and effect. There may be some conceit and self-satisfaction, but not without goodness of heart. The person indicated by this card must be a good sportsman and honest above all. The force in it does not tolerate contradiction nor delay, does not reason, but acts at once.

Eight of Pentacles

Divinatory Meanings: Work, employment, commission, craftsmanship, skill in craft and business, perhaps in the preparatory stage. A young man, or a dark girl.

Reversed: Voided ambition, vanity. It may also signify the possession of skill, in the sense of the ingenious mind turned to cunning and intrigue.

An artist in stone at his work, which he exhibits in the form of trophies. This has not much to do with useful work directly, nor with employment, but very much with skill and ingenuity. It gives skill and bravery, far above the average, outdoing the commonplace, neglecting fashion, sinning against tradition but widening the views and outlook. Dexterity will ensue from it. In matters of the heart it always tends to the unusual, superhuman, exotic, wayward, strange or dreamy. The illustration of the card is to be taken more as a warning against the dangers of this house than as a direct descriptive image of its nature; as a sort of hint: keep to your work, do not let yourself be led astray or misguided. It is also the house of the sick and the hospital. Charity comes under it.

That ambitions are wrecked in this house is correct in general, still the pentacles are never strong in any evil sense, and they are apt to wreck fortunes or bubble reputations rather than ambitions.

Seven of Pentacles

Divinatory Meanings: In the main, it is a card of business and barter. Altercation, quarrels. Innocence, ingenuity, purgation.

Reversed: Cause for anxiety regarding money which it may be proposed to lend. Impatience

A young man, leaning on his staff, looks intently at seven pentacles attached to a lump of greenery on his right; one would say that these were his treasures and that his heart was there.

In the main it contains friendly surroundings and is the house of traffic and business, of practical co-operation and interrelation. Aquarius is the house of the Angels too, and this may account perhaps for such renderings as innocence, and may mean that the individualistic and egotistic elements have to be modified into something more brotherly. What we have to do with the moon and its metal silver here, is less clear, unless the idea has been induced by the electric-blue color of this house, or by the fact that it is the first house of the lunar body in the solar system. Neither can we very clearly see why it should indicate riches, money, etc. This is probably a rather coarse transmission of the idea, that friendly relations together with the person's own good intentions and good-will must produce advantages in material things.

So the card indicates good business, profitable friendship, assistance and help of friends and vice versa; reliable and agreeable surroundings outside the family circle. The advantages will probably be the outcome of what has been sown before by good action.

Six of Pentacles

Divinatory Meanings: Presents, gifts, gratification. Attention, vigilance. Present prosperity.

Reversed: Desire, envy, jealousy, illusion.

A person in the guise of a merchant weighs money in a pair of scales and distributes it to the needy and distressed. It is a testimony to his own success in life, as well as to his goodness of heart.

The descriptions given by tradition are consequently correct and to the point. We may add, that here, in this combination, the heart's desire and wish, the impulses to speculate and to create, to make love and to do good, all become active and acute. So this must be a card of practical things, which for the greater part will be of a beneficial nature. Good action, which may include the fulfillment of duty as well as giving presents and alms. It means putting the heart into your action, working, acting, doing with much pleasure, conviction and self-confidence. This makes success almost certain. It means good-will and noble intention proved by gracious, charitable or useful action.

Five of Pentacles

Divinatory Meanings: Material trouble, destitution or otherwise. Love and lovers: wife, husband, friend, mistress. Conquest of fortune by reason.
Reversed: Disorder, chaos, ruin, discord, profligacy. Troubles in love.

Two mendicants in a snow-storm pass a lighted casement. It is the emanation of love, which brings the lover and the mistress (husband and wife, when regularized by law) and friends (when between persons of the same sex) sympathy and popularity, enthusiasm, hopefulness, love of traveling, roaming about, which in weaker cases easily leads to Bohemian habits, carelessness, disorder and so on. That the expansive nature indicated by this card causes material troubles above all, is evident, because it means that more is given out than received, which in matters of this material world does in fact bring troubles. But of a sort that may be easily forgiven, and helped, if not carried too far.

Four of Pentacles

Divinatory Meanings: The surety of possessions, cleaving to that which one has, gift, legacy, inheritance.

Reversed: Suspense, delay, opposition.

A crowned figure, having a pentacle over his crown, clasps another with hands and arms; two pentacles are under his feet. He holds to that which he has.

Secrets, the money and possessions of other people, death and sex, inheritance and debt, loans and delay in all material matters, psychic activity, but much hampering in all physical activities—all this makes clear much of what tradition has handed down. Everything falling in this house is connected with some secret, which cannot be divulged to the outer world, and consequently in relation to this world these things cannot appear in their full light or significance, are more or less handicapped, meet with obstacles and are wrongly judged. It is related to monastic life indeed. On the other hand it is the psychic and sexual expression of the love born in the heart, and it means, on this account certainly cleaving to that which one has in a very personal way.

It is the card of desire, attachment, secret longing for possession, which, when not being satisfied, may lead to retreat and retirement. The fire of the heart is here suffering from dissatisfaction or impossibility of realization. It is probably the least favorable card of the pentacles suit, at least in a material sense. It may hold much good for the future, however. Material benefit in this case will never go without some loss or sadness at the same time, as in the case of inheritance.

Three of Pentacles

Divinatory Meanings: Skilled labor. Nobility, aristocracy, renown, glory. Celebrity for an eldest son.

Reversed: Mediocrity in work. Pettiness, weakness.

A sculptor at his work in a monastery. Compare the design which illustrates the Eight of Pentacles. The apprentice or amateur therein has received his reward and is now at work in earnest.

The Fire on the Seventh house, which rules the contact of the Self and the Not-self, the relations between both, the executive ability in man. So this must lead to the idea of well-doing and noble demeanor, owing to the Sun and Venus again. Well-conducted relations denote civilization, aristocracy, and the proper expression of one's relation to the world in his occupation, his métier, profession, marriage and employment. So this card has to do with workmanship.

Aristocracy, good workmanship, skill, civil treatment and noblesse, agreeable relation, métier, employment, profession, marriage; good done to other people, bounty, profitable relations in business; restoration, reparation, beneficial arrangement. A marriage will do much good.

Two of Pentacles

Divinatory Meanings: A card of gaiety and recreation. News and messages in writing. Obstacles, agitation, trouble, embroilment—but more imagined than real. A difficult choice.

Reversed: Enforced gaiety, simulated enjoyment, literal sense, handwriting, composition, letters of exchange.

A young man, in the act of dancing, has a pentacle in either hand, and they are joined by that endless cord which is like the number 8 reversed. Infinite possibilities must naturally cause *embarras du choix*—the difficulty of choice—and the one possibility hindering the other; giving too much force and attention to little or subordinate things and persons. There can be very little harm, however, in any card of the pentacles suit; the greatest evil done here might be that too little profit is earned in proportion to the labour given to it.

On the other hand this card must necessarily mean good and conscientious work and fidelity of servants, agreeable and satisfactory work, reasonable remuneration, and consequently joy. The agreeable stimulation which it gives to the nervous system must cause gaiety and recreation. Good health is also one of the results.

Ace of Pentacles

Divinatory Meanings: The most favorable of all cards. Perfect contentment, ecstasy. Speedy intelligence. Gold.

Reversed: The evil side of wealth, bad intelligence. Great riches, prosperity, comfortable material conditions. A share in the finding of treasure.

A hand issuing from a cloud, holding up a pentacle. How could it be anything else but beneficial? The aces are all more or less a commencement of new prospects. The ace of pentacles indicates matters that will be beneficial and irresistible. It means the commencement of that what is wished for, desired, and this is what man calls his happiness. It is the spark of the Ego demonstrated in the practice of daily life; and this is what may well be called the note of good, which also brings good luck to other people. So there is creative energy in this card—not yet worked out into details, but originally decided and fairly sure to work out in the future in lucky events and prosperous happenings.

So there is promise in it and it is above all a card of good augury of a new and prosperous beginning. It is like a bright spark. Even among very bad cards it is the bright spark of hope and good-will, though of course in such cases it may be too weak to conquer adverse circumstances immediately. It may mean further a person or thing of first ranking.

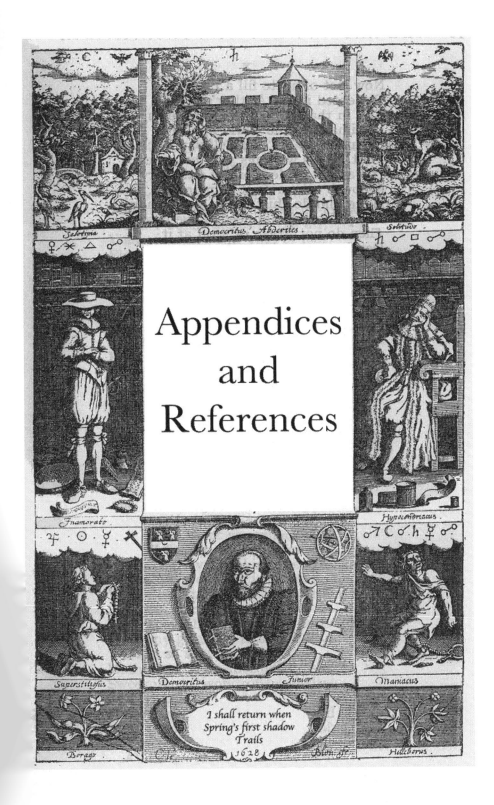

Appendices
and
References

I shall return when
Spring's first shadow
Trails

Appendix 1 – Tarot Spreads

The art of divination with the Tarot lends itself greatly to personal preference and improvisation with the cards. There are as many different decks and ways to interpret the cards as there are cartomancers attempting to divine the future. Each card reader must seek out their own path and find their own best way of divining the meaning of the Tarot. No one way is better or more accurate than any other. It varies from person to person and some cartomancers have different decks that they use for different types of readings. There are also specialty Tarot decks that have been designed with a particular spread in mind. When developing your own method of divination, although complicated spreads can yield significant detail in the reading, consider the words of A.E. Waite: "Simplicity is the way of truth."

These spreads are presented as an introduction to the simplest (and most popular) ways of laying out the cards. However, cartomancers are free to adapt the spreads to their own liking.

THE CELTIC CROSS

The cartomancer first selects a card to represent the person (or matter) about which inquiry is made. This card is called the SIGNIFICATOR. Should you wish to ascertain something in connection with yourself, take the card with which you feel the strongest connection. Having selected the Significator, place it on the table, face upwards. Then shuffle and cut the rest of the pack three times, keeping the faces of the cards downwards, while pondering the question at hand.

Turn up the top or FIRST CARD of the pack; cover the Significator with it, and say: "This covers him." This card shows the influence which is affecting the person or matter of inquiry. The atmosphere in which the other currents work.

Turn up the SECOND CARD and lay it across the FIRST, saying. "This crosses him." It shows the nature of the obstacles in the matter. If it is a favorable card, the opposing forces will not be serious, or it may indicate that something good in itself will not be productive of good in the particular situation.

Turn up the THIRD CARD; place it above the Significator, and say: "This crowns him." It represents (a) the Querent's aim or ideal in the matter; (b) the best that can be achieved under the circumstances, but that which has not yet been made actual.

Turn up the FOURTH CARD; place it below the Significator, and say: "This is beneath him." It shows the foundation or basis of the matter, that which has already passed into actuality and which the Significator has made his own. It can also represent skill or talent that the Querent possesses which will be beneficial in the situation.

Turn up the FIFTH CARD; place it on the side of the Significator from which is looking away, and say: "This is behind him." It shows the influence that is just passed, or is now passing away.

Turn up the SIXTH CARD; place it on the side that the Significator is facing, and say: "This is before him." It shows the influence that is coming into action and will operate in the near future.

Turn up the SEVENTH CARD; it signifies himself—that is, the Significator—whether person or thing, and shows its position or attitude in the circumstances.

The EIGHTH CARD signifies his house, that is, his environment and the tendencies at work which have an effect on the matter—for instance, his position in life, the influence of immediate friends and family. The people who surround him.

The NINTH CARD gives his hopes or fears in the matter.

The TENTH is what will come, the final result, the culmination which is brought about by the influences shown by the other cards. It is on this card that the Querent should concentrate his intuitive faculties in respect to the divinatory meanings of the spread. It should embody whatsoever has been divined from the other cards on the table, and might fall like sparks from heaven if the card should happen to be from the Major Arcana.

If it should happen that the last card is of a dubious nature, from which no final decision can be drawn, repeat the operation, taking in this case the Tenth Card as the Significator. The pack must be again shuffled and cut three times and the first ten cards laid out as before. By this a more detailed account of "What will come" may be obtained.

If the Tenth Card should be a Court Card, it shows that the subject of the divination falls ultimately into the hands of a person represented by that card, and its end depends mainly on them. In this event also it is useful to take the Court Card in question as the Significator in a fresh operation, and discover what is the nature of its influence in the matter.

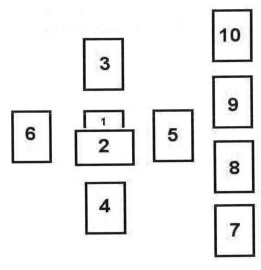

THE ELEMENTAL PENTACLE

Each position of the cards will signify one of the five elements. Their proximity to one another will potentially weaken or strengthen the influence of the cards in corresponding positions. The pentagram coaxes the cards into a relationship with one another, giving elemental context to the reading and providing a complete circle, like the world itself.

1. Upper Point - Spirit

Similar to the Tenth Card in the Celtic Cross, this card represents a synthesis of all the other cards and is the key to the reading. It also represents the overall outcome of the situation. This card is more powerful if it is from the Major Arcana and in any case, it is not weakened or strengthened by any other card.

2. Lower Left Point - Earth

This card represents the foundation of the matter, showing why things are the way they are. This position is strengthened if it's a Pentacle, and weakened if a Sword. This card is influenced by the card in the Air position.

3. Upper Right Point - Water

This card represents changing situations which are coming in the future. This position is strengthened if it's a Cup, and weakened if a Wand. This card is influenced by the card in the Fire position.

4. Upper Left Point - Air

This card reveals a secret to the Querent, showing them what they must learn in order to act. This position is strengthened if it's a Sword, and weakened if a Pentacle. This card is influenced by the card in the Earth position.

5. Lower Right Point - Fire

This card shows what the Querent must do in order to have the best possible outcome. This position is strengthened if it's a Wand, and weakened if a Cup. This card is influenced by the card in the Water position.

THREE CARD SPREAD

The primary advantage to the Three Card spread is its simplicity. Ask a question and the three cards will give a clear picture of what the Querent is facing and what can be expected in the future. The primary failure of this spread is that is does not suggest an action for the Querent to take, but this may be acceptable when all that is sought is a general feeling for the situation. Along with the Celtic Cross, this spread is one of the most popular because it is quick and easy to interpret.

The only easier spread would be a one-card draw, which can also provide surprisingly accurate results!

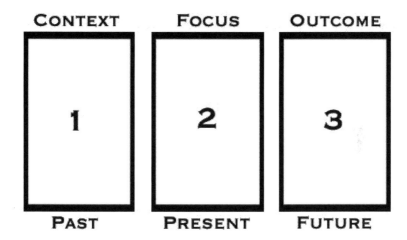

Appendix 2 – Tarot Decks

THE CARY SHEET

(1500 – 1550 from a woodcut block print. Possibly from Milan.)

THE MARSEILLES DECK

(1701 – 1715 by Jean Dodal, although numerous versions exist.)

(Early 1500s from a woodcut block print. Author unknown.)

THE RIDER-WAITE-SMITH DECK

(1909 by Arthur Edward Waite and Pamela Colman Smith.)

References

TEXTS

Ouspensky, P. D. *The Symbolism of the Tarot: Philosophy of Occultism in Pictures and Numbers; Pen-pictures of the Twenty Two Tarot Cards*. Trans. A. L. Pogossky. St. Petersburg: Trood Print. and Pub., 1913.

Papus. *The Tarot of the Bohemians: The Most Ancient Book in the World. For the Exclusive Use of Initiates*. Trans. A. P. Morton. London: Chapman and Hall, 1892.

Thierens, A. E. *The General Book of the Tarot: Containing the Astrological Key to the Tarot-System*. London: W. Rider, 1928.

Waite, Arthur Edward. *The Pictorial Key to the Tarot: Being Fragments of a Secret Tradition under the Veil of Divination*. London: W. Rider, 1911.

DECKS

The Tarot of Charles VI by Pellegrino Prisciani (1400 or earlier)

The Visconti Tarot – *Visconti di Modrone* – Cary Yale Deck commissioned by Filippo Maria Visconti, Duke of Milan (1442 – 1447)

The Visconti Tarot – Pierpont Morgan Bergamo Deck commissioned by Filippo Maria Visconti, Duke of Milan (1451)

The Tarot of Marseilles by Jean Dodal (1701 – 1715)

The Tarot of Marseilles by Bernardin Suzanne (1839)

The Rider-Waite-Smith deck by A.E. Waite and Pamela Colman Smith (1909)

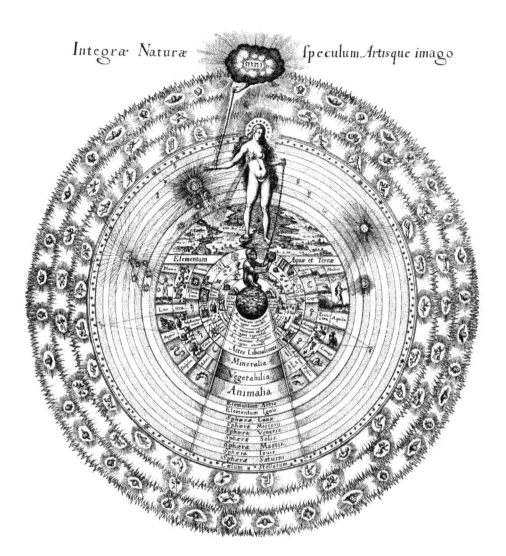

Integræ Naturæ Speculum, Artisque imago

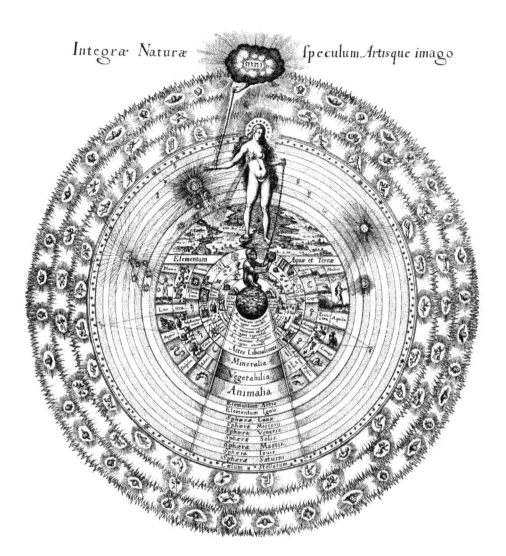

Made in the
USA
Columbia, SC